395/
1

1

SOCIAL SCIENCE SEMINAR SERIES

Raymond H. Muessig and Vincent R. Rogers, Editors

THE VOLUMES AND THE AUTHORS

The Study of Anthropology, Pertti J. Pelto

Political Science: An Informal Overview, Francis J. Sorauf

Geography: Its Scope and Spirit, Jan O. M. Broek

Sociology: The Study of Man in Society, Caroline B. Rose

The Nature and the Study of History, Henry Steele Commager

Economics and Its Significance, Richard S. Martin and
  Reuben G. Miller

THE CONSULTANTS FOR THE SERIES

Anthropology, George D. Spindler

Political Science, Charles S. Hyneman

Geography, Jan O. M. Broek

Sociology, Arnold M. Rose

History, Henry Steele Commager

Economics, Kenneth E. Boulding

THE STUDY OF ANTHROPOLOGY

Pertti J. Pelto
Department of Anthropology
University of Minnesota

With a Concluding Chapter Suggesting Methods
for Elementary and Secondary Teachers
by Raymond H. Muessig and Vincent R. Rogers

Consultant
George D. Spindler
Department of Anthropology
Stanford University

CHARLES E. MERRILL BOOKS, INC.   COLUMBUS, OHIO

To Pat, Gina, Joshua, and Dunja,

Who all had a hand in this work

Social Science Seminar Series

Edited By
Raymond H. Muessig
and
Vincent R. Rogers

The Social Science Seminar Series presents scholarly viewpoints on and information about history, geography, political science, economics, sociology, and anthropology. This social science material is complemented by creative and practical methods, tailored to each of the individual fields, for elementary and secondary teachers.

One assumption built into these six volumes is that the social studies program in our schools should reflect more faithfully and sensitively the social sciences from which it is derived. It is imperative, then, that social scientists contribute their suggestions regarding over-all content selection problems in the social studies.

A second premise inherent in the Social Science Seminar Series is that professional educators are responsible for translating appropriate social science substance into meaningful and enriching learning experiences for children and youth. In their contacts with the editors of this Series, the contributing social scientists repeatedly made the point that they could discuss their disciplines only as they saw them and not in the light of what should be done with them in the schools. It is the professional educator—thoroughly prepared and broadly experienced in thinking about and coping with educational theories, problems, and practices—who must weld a framework that will support understandings, skills, attitudes, and appreciations drawn from or tied to the social science disciplines. It is the educator, too, who must decide what can and should be taught at various grade levels and how this subject matter might be conveyed, buttressed, and assessed by a myriad of suitable methods, materials, resources, and evaluative processes.

There is a critical need in both pre-service and in-service teacher education programs for up-to-date, clear, stimulating material concerned with recent developments in the social sciences. Teachers should see these disciplines as spheres of continuing scientific study and inquiry, rather than as hardened, static, sterile bodies of accumulated fact. Further, they must obtain a more sophisticated grasp of the goals, scope, importance, and interpretation of these fields as well as some understanding of the concerns faced by those working in a given field. The Social Science Seminar Series encourages and assists teachers at all instructional levels to critically examine their purposes and approaches to the teaching of specific areas of content fundamentally related to the disciplines treated.

With this perspective in mind, the editors of the Series suggested that each of the contributing social scientists ask himself what his field really did contain that professional educators should consider teaching to youngsters. Each author was asked to describe the nature of his field; to trace briefly its history, development, and maturation; and to look at its unique methods of working as well as those procedures shared with other social sciences and related fields. Most importantly, each specialist was requested to select out of mountains of data a series of fundamental, compelling ideas that have emerged from his field.

In each volume of the Social Science Seminar Series, the editors have written a final chapter to accompany the discussions and analyses of the social scientists. The editors have *not* attempted to build an overarching theory of social studies education; rather, they have concentrated upon specific, functional classroom methods. The concluding chapters in this Series, therefore, do not present a total program, a master theory, a blanket plan of attack, or an endorsement of the proposals of any single group endeavoring to improve social studies instruction. The generalizations the editors have chosen to illustrate should not be viewed as the basis for a course or sequence of offerings. The ideas they have introduced transcend particular topics, units, themes, or curricula. Careful exposure to them can support many learnings. The editors have not dealt at this time with *why, how much, where,* and *when* questions regarding the place of individual social sciences in the social studies family today or tomorrow. As they see it, each social science can be taught by itself in breadth or depth, woven into existing scope and sequence patterns for development or supplementary purposes, or assigned manifold roles in some yet-to-be-developed curriculum design.

Space limitations have not permitted the exhaustive treatment of a single idea, problem, or approach drawn from each of the social sciences represented. Instead, the editors have suggested a number of procedures that could be used or adapted for use in a variety of elementary and secondary school situations. It is not intended that the techniques offered in the Series be employed in a one-a-day, isolated, disjointed, decontextualized fashion. A superficial flitting from one major insight to another would have little meaning for students and would possess limited retention or transfer value. It is not expected that pupils will comprehend abstract generalizations in a definitive sense after an occasional lesson or two. The editors believe that global ideas should be approached, discovered, introduced, developed, and confirmed in different ways and contexts and at increased levels of complexity throughout the school years. They have taken into account the fact that it takes time, patience, and systematic organization to build durable learning.

The Social Science Seminar Series, then, should function as a point of embarkation—inspiring and challenging readers to keep abreast of developments in the social sciences and in social studies education.

Preface

In his eloquent book, *Mirror for Man*, Clyde Kluckhohn observed, "Anthropology is no longer just the science of the long-ago and far away." This statement is even more true today than when it was written in 1949. Anthropologists have maintained a continuing interest in the past; yet the present also commands their attention both at home and in places regarded as remote not too long ago, with names that may still sound strange to some people. In an age of breathtaking innovations in transportation and communication and increased personal contacts among the inhabitants of this fascinating planet, the anthropologist has earned attention and respect. Contemporary anthropology is a scientific horn of plenty, brimming with unique, penetrating insights worthy of consideration.

We believe that carefully selected products and processes—or ideas and ways of thinking and working—identified with anthropology can be apprehended to varying degrees by many learners. This book is the culmination of the extended, cooperative efforts of an anthropologist and two social studies educators. The first five chapters on the field itself were written by Dr. Pertti J. Pelto of the Department of Anthropology at the University of Minnesota. Dr. Pelto deals with the birth and growth of anthropology, its relationship to other social sciences, and its interests, theories, endeavors, and findings. The reader will find that Dr. Pelto has also recommended numerous sources for independent study which would be interesting and enriching. The last chapter on classroom methodology was written by Dr. Raymond H. Muessig of the College of Education at The Ohio State University and Dr. Vincent R. Rogers of the College of Education at the University of Minnesota. Focusing on a group of basic generalizations drawn from Dr. Pelto's preceding five chapters, Professor Muessig and Professor Rogers propose and illustrate numerous approaches teachers could employ to help elementary and secondary school students gain some understanding and feeling for these important anthropological observations. Dr. George D. Spindler of the Department of Anthropology at Stanford University served as academic consultant for this volume.

The Editors

Table
of
Contents

            by **Raymond H. Muessig and Vincent R. Rogers,**
            81

            Introduction, 81
            Anthropological Generalizations and Methodological
              Illustrations, 81–116
            Conclusion, 116

chapter one

The Study of Man

By the beginning of the twentieth century the scholars who interested themselves in the unusual, dramatic, and puzzling aspects of man's history were known as anthropologists. They were the men who were searching for man's most remote ancestors; for Homer's Troy; for the original home of the American Indian; for the relationship between bright sunlight and skin color; for the origin of the wheel, safety pins, and pottery. They wanted to know "how modern man got that way": why some people are ruled by a king, some by old men, others by warriors, and none by women; why some peoples pass on property in the male line, others in the female line, still others equally to heirs of both sexes; why some people fall sick and die when they think they are bewitched, and others laugh at the idea. They sought for the universals in human biology and in human conduct. They proved that men of different continents and regions were physically much more alike than they were different. They discovered many parallels in human customs, some of which could be explained by historical contact. In other words, anthropology had become the science of human similarities and differences.[1]

The broadest and boldest definition of anthropology states simply that "anthropology is the study of man and his works." And, in fact, only that very broad definition can include all the varied field studies, theoretical interests, and teaching areas of people who call themselves anthropologists. Under the title "Anthropology" in the course catalogues of major universities, we

[1] Clyde Kluckhohn, *Mirror for Man* (New York: McGraw-Hill Book Co., Inc., 1949), p. 2.

1

notice first that this field of study is usually divided into two main branches—physical anthropology and cultural (or social) anthropology. Most anthropology departments offer two separate introductory courses corresponding to these two aspects of the study of man.

PHYSICAL ANTHROPOLOGY

Ever since the great Swedish naturalist Linnaeus published his monumental classification of plants and animals in the eighteenth century, man has been listed among the animals, and the study of man has been regarded as a branch of natural science. An important aspect of biological anthropology is the examination of the many-sided evidence for the evolution of man from "lower" forms of animal life. Therefore, introductory courses in physical anthropology often begin with materials on the comparative anatomy of *Homo sapiens* and his nearest "cousins," the apes and monkeys, all fellow members of the order of mammals called *Primates*. Then they may study the fossil evidence of human evolution in the form of fossilized bones of Neandertal Man, Java Man and a great number of other fragments from men and ape-men that lived hundreds of thousands of years ago. Interest in man's biological relationships with the other primates also leads to a comparative study of the social behavior of subhuman primates, such as the gorillas, chimpanzees, and baboons.

The variations among different physical populations of *Homo sapiens*, commonly divided into Mongoloid, Negroid, Caucasoid and several smaller racial stocks, are another major concern of the physical anthropologists. Recent developments in the science of genetics have changed the study of racial classifications from a dull cataloguing of obvious traits (color of skin, eye color, head shape, height, etc.) into an exciting search for patterns in the genetic inheritance of blood types, resistance to particular diseases, and examination of biological adaptation to different world climates.

In addition to these two relatively well-known lines of interest, physical anthropology has become increasingly concerned with the study of human growth and constitution, relationships of nutrition to body build, and a number of other physiological problems that bring anthropology into close contact with the special fields of anatomy, radiobiology, serology, physiology, and general medicine.

CULTURAL (SOCIAL) ANTHROPOLOGY

The distinctive feature that makes man so different from other animals is that the human pattern of life is based on "culture,"—socially learned patterns of behavior, based on symbolic processes. Other animals may have some rudiments of culture, but for man *all* behavior is pervasively cultural. The several different facets of human culture (culture history, language, social structures, personality, etc.) give rise to a series of subfields that may be grouped in a variety of ways in the teaching of anthropology.

Archaeology

Archaeology is sometimes grouped with physical anthropology for teaching purposes. It is clearly cultural rather than biological, however, for the archaeologist studies the information about human cultures that can be gained from the careful digging up of ancient dwellings, monuments, objects of art, tools, weapons, and other works of man covered over by the soils of time.

Typical course offerings in archaeology can include: "New World Archaeology" (concerned with the prehistoric remains of American Indian cultures); "Old World Prehistory" (study of the stone tools, cave art, and other evidence about human life during the million or more years of the great Ice Ages); "Beginnings of Near Eastern Civilization"; and various specializations within these broad studies.

Since archaeologists are concerned with "digging up man's past," they have important connections with history and historians. As a matter of fact, the "classical archaeologists," who dig in the ruins of ancient civilizations of the Mediterranean and Middle East (Troy, Crete, the tombs of Egypt, etc.), are usually found in departments of history or the classics, rather than in anthropology. Concern with the evidence of the past found in the earth's crust also links archaeologists with geologists, palaeontologists, palaeobotanists, and the geophysicists.

Linguistics

"Linguistics" is the study of language—man's highly elaborated system of communication. This study is not concerned with learning to speak foreign languages fluently but rather is aimed at accurate scientific description and comparison of languages. Probably the earliest strong interest in linguistics was developed around the study of the relationships among languages, particularly when it was discovered that most of the languages of Europe, though mutually unintelligible, are descended from a single common ancestor language—ancient Indo-European.

Recent developments in linguistics have brought the linguists into increasing contact with psychologists, philosophers, and mathematicians, as they pursue such topics as psycholinguistics, metalinguistics, semantics, and communications theory.

Ethnology

"Peoples and Cultures of Africa," "Ethnology of Oceania," "North American Indians" and a number of similar course titles illustrate the cultural anthropologist's concern with the infinite varieties of human behavior that have been found on the face of our globe. From this world-wide range of cultures and peoples, anthropologists search for similarities and differences that provide clues to understanding "human nature" and human culture history.

The courses in which cultural anthropologists present their systematic comparisons and theoretical researches are variously entitled "Comparative Economics," "Comparative Religion," "Culture Change," "Primitive Law and Government," "Social Structure," and so on. When psychological theory is systematically interwoven with these comparative ethnological data, we find courses entitled "Culture and Personality" and "Psychological Anthropology."

Whenever an anthropologist is engaged in straightforward description of the cultural patterns of a given society he is concerned with "ethnography." When his materials are organized in terms of social systems, we can label the research (or the course) "Social Anthropology," indicating (among other things) the influence on Americans of some very interesting developments in British anthropology of the past forty years. Other diverse interests of anthropologists are made clear by the names of their course listings: for example, "Ethnomusicology," "Comparative Folklore," and "Primitive Art." Courses in which anthropological knowledge and theory are centered on the practical problems of our complex age are usually titled "Applied Anthropology."

ANTHROPOLOGY IS FUNDAMENTALLY CROSS-CULTURAL

Very often the first sign of an anthropologist-to-be is a young boy's or girl's fascination with Indians, lost continents, explorations in Africa, and exotic island peoples of the South Seas. The same kind of fascination with the "unusual" and "different" among peoples and cultures has spurred many anthropologists to their first extensive field work. When a thirst for systematic observation and comparative research are grafted onto the earlier romantic impulses, the motivations for a mature anthropology begin to emerge.

Curiosity and fascination with the exotic are not the main justifications for the anthropologist's interests in primitive peoples,[2] however. The more fundamental explanation is that non-Western societies provide a great range of behavioral diversity. Economic institutions, family organization, religious beliefs and practices, magic, artistic achievements, and personality types of every description provide the evidence for establishing the constants and the variants of human culture. The anthropologist feels that the fundamental principles of cultural and social systems can be discovered only through study of the whole range of human behavior patterns. Still another reason for the anthropologist's study of non-Western societies is that these provide him with a sort of "laboratory" setting, where something approaching the total scope of a cultural system can be observed in a relatively compact, localized community that is not just a fragment of a huge, modern society.

Some anthropologists have maintained that their field of study is concerned exclusively with primitive peoples, but most anthropologists see their discipline as a general study of bio-cultural man; and recent anthropological research has diverged sharply from the earlier concentration on pre-literate societies. A very large part of the anthropological research of the postwar period has been in the subcommunities and specialized segments of large, literate

---

[2] The word "primitive" in casual conversation seems to refer most usually to peoples and practices that "civilized" Europeans and Americans regard as strange, quaint, and (generally) inferior. The anthropologist, when he uses the expression at all, defines "primitive peoples" as people who have no written language—hence, "pre-literate" people. Anthropological researchers generally avoid making value judgments about supposedly "inferior" or "irrational" or "backward" behavior.

societies. These include work on rural communities of modern
Europe, Latin America, Japan, and India, in addition to anthropological study of topics like "the culture of a psychiatric hospital,"
"city taverns," "themes in French culture," and "the American
kinship system."

THE INTEGRATION OF ANTHROPOLOGY

It is evident that anthropology—however specific it may often be
in dealing with data—aims at being ultimately a co-ordinating
science, somewhat as a legitimate holding corporation co-ordinates
constituent companies. We anthropologists will never know China
as intensively as a Sinologist does, or prices, credit, and banking as
well as an economist, or heredity with the fulness of the genetic
biologist. But we face what these more intensive scholars only glance
at intermittently and tangentially, if at all: to try to understand in
some measure how Chinese civilization and economics and human
heredity, and some dozens of other highly developed special bodies
of knowledge, do indeed interrelate in being all parts of "man"—
flowing out of man, centered in him, products of him.[3]

With these words the late Alfred L. Kroeber, one of the foremost anthropologists of this century, expressed the idea that the
stuff of anthropology is drawn from many different areas of knowledge. The research interests and types of courses taught by anthropologists reflect this great diversity, but in many situations
today there are tendencies toward the fragmentation of the
discipline. Physical anthropology, for example, is becoming increasingly specialized and complex in its researches on the physiology,
anatomy, and genetic attributes of man. Most cultural anthropologists find themselves farther and farther out of touch with the
newest research and information in this field. At the same time,
scholars in physical anthropology experience great pressures to
concentrate their energies on the rapidly developing areas of
radiobiology, the chemistry and physics of human genetics, and
related fields. Thus they may become comparative strangers to
the interests and researches of the linguists, cultural anthropologists, and archaeologists who are their fellow staff members in
departments of anthropology.

Also, the study of linguistics has become highly specialized,
with an intricate vocabulary of description, semimathematical

---

[3] A. L. Kroeber (ed.), *Anthropology Today* (Chicago: University of Chicago
Press, 1953), p. xiv. Copyright 1953. All rights reserved.

modes of analysis of language structure, and extremely complex philosophical and psychological arguments over fundamental assumptions in the field.

As we view the natural history of different branches of science and philosophy, we see that diversification and separation of fields of study is a natural result of increased knowledge about the world in which we live. It is easy, therefore, to argue that gradual splitting up of the different branches of anthropology into separate disciplines would be just as natural as the differentiation of chemistry, physics, and biology from the earlier unity of general science. But most anthropologists, especially in the United States, cling stubbornly to the "holistic principle" as stated by Dr. Kroeber. For, despite all tendencies toward specialization, the strong interrelatedness of man's physical characteristics and his behavioral systems cannot be ignored. From whatever angle the nature of the human animal is approached, there is no denying that man's economic behavior, religious institutions, and other aspects of culture are deeply influenced by his psychobiological characteristics. Similarly, man's body as a physical system is affected by his religion, his occupation, his family, and other social and cultural facts.

One area of study that graphically illustrates the integration of the study of man is concerned with the problems of mental illness. In postwar years important advances have been made in the development of a holistic theory of psychiatric disorder. The development of drugs and other organic treatments demonstrates the relationship of man's biological attributes to his psychological functioning. Theoretical developments in the area of psychosomatic medicine offer additional evidence of these linkages. At the same time, studies of mental disorders among the Eskimos, peoples in Africa, Asia, and other areas, and evidence of different rates and kinds of mental illness in subsections of our own society show the importance of social and cultural factors in problems of mental health.

The integration of biological and cultural data in research on mental illness is particularly well illustrated in Anthony F. C. Wallace's analysis of a mental disorder called *pibloktoq*, found among the Greenland Eskimos. *Pibloktoq* is characterized by compulsive mimicking behavior, "speaking in tongues," shouting, weeping, tearing off clothing, and running away naked in the arctic cold. Rejecting a wholly psychoanalytic interpretation for this disorder, Wallace suggests that it is related to periodic calcium deficiencies in the Eskimo diet. Particular social circumstances trigger the breakdown, however, and the specific contents of the aberrant behavior must be understood in terms of Eskimo psychological and cultural patterns. Clearly, research on problems of this sort requires close collaboration among biological, psychological, and cultural sciences.

RELATIONSHIPS WITH OTHER SOCIAL SCIENCES

In practice there is a good deal of both theoretical and practical overlap between anthropology and sociology. And the areas of common interest seem to have increased considerably in the past fifteen or twenty years. Nonetheless, some general differences separate the interests of *most* anthropologists from those of *most* sociologists. These differences in tendency include:

1. Most anthropologists prefer to study non-Western peoples (though there are many exceptions); most sociologists prefer to study aspects of Western society and culture. (But growing numbers of sociologists are now immersed in studies of African, Indian, Chinese, and other societies, and more anthropologists are looking at their own cultures.)
2. Most anthropologists prefer to do research on small communities, by means of observations and interviews of people in face-to-face contact. Most sociologists prefer to study larger segments of social systems, using information gathered on questionnaires or extracted from statistics on population, crime rates, employment figures, voting records, and so on. In general, sociologists feel much more at home using statistical analysis than do anthropologists.
3. Anthropologists include physical anthropology as an important part of their science; sociologists concentrate their studies nearly exclusively on social aspects of man.
4. Most anthropologists consider human culture history to be a central concern of the discipline; the majority of sociologists leave historical studies to others, preferring modern social institutions for research topics.

The differences between anthropology and psychology are much more clearly observable, though again there are growing areas of overlap. Psychologists usually study the behavior of individuals in carefully defined laboratory or experimental situations; thus, psychology is much more an experimental science than is anthropology. Psychologists are, in the main, even less interested than sociologists in study of non-Western peoples. However, the rapidly developing field of social psychology includes cross-cultural studies and other features that are very close to the interests of psychologically-oriented anthropologists. Anthropologists and psychologists also have common interests and much potential for joint research on the physiology of the human brain and nervous system. A somewhat unexpected area of co-operation has developed between psychology and anthropology in laboratory and field studies of monkeys and apes.

Anthropology also shares notable similarities of interest with geography. Studies of the spread of domestication of plants and animals; adaptation of peoples to particular kinds of physical environments; social and cultural characteristics of pastoral (animal herding) societies, and a great many other areas of research are studied simultaneously by geographers and anthropologists. In topics such as Islamic culture history, Chinese culture and society, and Latin American culture history we often find anthropologists and historians working on very similar research interests, though methods of study may be different. The full range of anthropological interests and research links the work of anthropologists with that of scholars in many other fields. This is natural and expected, for all scholars accept the principle of the interconnection of the universe, the unity of all life on earth, and the oneness of human history and society. Special areas of study labeled with the names of various "ologies" are, after all, artificial segments of information chopped out of the unified web of events and things. If scholars paid careful heed to the artificial boundaries between areas of study, we might still be in the Dark Ages of human knowledge.

SUMMARY

Since anthropology is "the study of man," including human social, cultural, psychological, and physical characteristics, anthropological study is partly biological science, partly social science, and in part included among the humanities. In the main lines of their studies, anthropologists may be distinguishable from sociologists, psychologists, physiologists, zoologists, geographers, historians, and others; but the wide-ranging interests of individual scholars make any clear boundaries among these several disciplines impossible to draw. Some of the most exciting areas of modern research are those that play havoc with the boundaries among the various disciplines. Studies of mental health and mental disorder, for example, involve the work of physiologists, psychiatrists, psychologists, sociologists, anthropologists, geneticists, biochemists, and social workers. The general areas of human evolution and cultural history similarly combine work from dozens of different branches of science and humanities.

In the welter of interlaced scientific and historical studies anthropologists have attempted to maintain a broad, holistic approach to their work. Narrow specializations have generally been avoided, and the splitting of anthropology into separated subcompartments has also been avoided, although the strains involved in this unity of anthropology sometimes show on the faces of weary and harassed students who must spread their studies over such wide ranges of knowledge.

Suggested Reading

Hoebel, E. Adamson. *Man in the Primitive World* (2nd ed.). New York: McGraw-Hill Book Co., Inc., 1958.

Written as an elementary college textbook, this work is extremely well illustrated and exciting reading. The major sub-areas of anthropology are discussed, and important concepts and information in each area are presented simply and clearly.

*Kluckhohn, Clyde. *Mirror For Man.* New York: Fawcett Publications, Inc., 1960.

This is a well-rounded, readable introduction to anthropology written by one of the most prominent anthropologists of recent decades.

*Oliver, Douglas. *Invitation to Anthropology.* ("American Museum Science Books.") Garden City: The Natural History Press, 1964.

Dr. Oliver explains very briefly and succinctly the fundamental ideas, methods, and schools of thought in modern anthropology.

---

* Paperback.

Advanced Reading

*Kroeber, A. L. *Anthropology, Biology and Race*, Vol. I. *Anthropology, Culture Patterns and Processes*, Vol. II. New York: Harbinger Paperbacks, 1963.

This classic compendium by "the grand old man" of anthropology was first published in 1948, but is far from out of date.

*Tax, Sol (ed.). *Anthropology Today—Selections*. Chicago: University of Chicago Press, 1962.

These "inventory papers" on various aspects of anthropological method and theory were put together for a high-level conference in 1953. Although much has happened in anthropology since that time, the collection gives an impressive survey of the state of anthropology in the postwar period.

chapter two

The
History of
Anthropology

ANTHROPOLOGY AMONG THE ANCIENTS

They have, however, one singular custom in which they differ from every other nation in the world. They take the mother's and not the father's name. Ask a Lycian who he is, and he answers by giving his own name, that of his mother, and so on in the female line. Moreover, if a free woman marry a man who is a slave, their children are full citizens; but if a free man marry a foreign woman or live with a concubine, even though he be the first person in the state, the children forfeit all the rights of citizenship.[1]

This concise description of a matrilineal, or "mother-right," social system is from the ethnological observations of Herodotus, the Greek historian, philosopher, and anthropologist (484–424 B.C.).

Herodotus traveled widely in the then known world, and he observed firsthand many different peoples and customs. Like modern anthropologists, he interviewed "key informants" and recorded their statements for posterity.

Concerning ethnocentrism, Herodotus wrote:

. . . if one were to offer men to choose out of all the customs in the world such as seemed to them best, they would examine the whole number, and end by preferring their own; so convinced are they that their own usages far surpass those of all others . . .[2]

---

[1] E. H. Blakeney (ed.), *The History of Herodotus*, 2 vols., trans. George Rawlinson (London: Everyman's Library, 1910), I, 89.
[2] *Ibid.*, pp. 229–30.

Although Herodotus and a few other ancient Greeks were the first men to embark on a naturalistic study of man, we must turn to the Roman, Tacitus, for our best example of an early "ethnographic monograph" about a particular "primitive" culture. In his *Germania* (98 A.D.) Tacitus described the character, manners, and geographical setting of the German tribes. He wrote to warn fellow Romans of the strength and spirit of the Germans, for he saw them as uncorrupted barbarians who would bring about the downfall of a rapidly degenerating Rome. He noted with admiration that "no one in Germany finds vice amusing, or calls it 'up-to-date' to debauch and be debauched." [3] Also:

> For all that, marriage in Germany is austere, and there is no feature in their morality that deserves higher praise. They are almost unique among barbarians in being satisfied with one wife each. The exceptions, which are exceedingly rare, are of men who receive offers of many wives because of their rank. There is no question of sexual passion. The dowry is brought by husband to wife, not by wife to husband. [4]

After Tacitus, up to the thirteenth and fourteenth centuries, there appeared few men who attempted dispassionate observation and explanation of human behavior and society. The development of a strong religious movement, dating from St. Augustine, drew men toward more theological and metaphysical interpretations of human behavior. Any naturalistic, empirical investigation of man's nature and surroundings came to be discouraged by threats of harassment and persecution.

THE GREAT TRAVELERS: MARCO POLO, IBN BATUTA, IBN KHALDUN

In the thirteenth and fourteenth centuries there were a few isolated instances of "proto-anthropological" writing. The famous Marco Polo, having traveled in China and much of the rest of Asia for more than twenty years (1271-1295), transmitted to posterity a wealth of knowledge of peoples and customs far beyond the imaginations of his Italian contemporaries. Here is a fragment from his observations about the Tartars of Central Asia:

---

[3] *Tacitus on Britain and Germany*, trans. H. Mattingly (London: Penguin Classics, 1948), p. 117.
[4] *Ibid.*, p. 115.

They have circular houses made of wood and covered with felt, which they carry with them on four-wheeled wagons wherever they go. For the framework of rods is so neatly and skillfully constructed that it is light to carry . . . and I assure you that the womenfolk buy and sell and do all that is needful for their husbands and households. For the men do not bother themselves with anything but hunting and warfare and falconry . . . They have no objection to eating the flesh of horses and dogs and drinking mare's milk . . . Not for anything in the world would one of them touch another's wife; they are too well assured that such a deed is wrongful and disgraceful . . .[5]

Ibn Batuta (1304-1378), the greatest Arab traveler of the Middle Ages, set off from his native North Africa on a series of travels to Russia, China, India, Sumatra, Cambodia, and then into sub-Saharan West Africa, including Timbuktu. The main lines of his twenty-eight years of travel covered something like 75,000 miles. Then by royal order he dictated his narrative to Mohammed Ibn Juzai. Ibn Batuta's narrative reveals much information about relationships among the various Islamic governments of his time, as well as details of Islamic religious and cultural practices.

About the same time, another Arab scholar, Ibn Khaldun, was collecting observations and writing about the nature of human society. He was not just a collector of information and observations, like Polo and Ibn Batuta, but must be considered a profound social scientist. From his own rich experiences in various Islamic governments, plus his extensive reading and observations, he attempted to organize "a study of human society in all its different forms, the nature and characteristics of each of these forms, and the laws governing its development." [6] Some of Ibn Khaldun's principles are remarkably modern, though written over 500 years ago:

1. Social phenomena obey laws, which are sufficiently constant to cause social events to follow regular, well-defined patterns and sequences.
2. These laws operate on masses, and cannot be significantly influenced by isolated individuals. (He gives the example of the reformer's attempts to rejuvenate a corrupt state. These reform efforts meet with little success; the individual's efforts are submerged by overwhelming social forces.)

[5] *The Travels of Marco Polo*, trans. R. E. Latham (London: Penguin Classics, 1958), p. 67.
[6] *An Arab Philosophy of History*, trans. and arr. by Charles Issawi (London: John Murray, 1950), pp. 7–9.

3. Social laws can be discovered only by gathering large numbers of facts, from which sequences and correlations can be observed.
4. Similar social laws operate in societies of the same kind of structures, however separated in time and space. (He notes similarities among nomadic Bedouins, Kurds, and Berbers.)
5. Societies are not static, for social forms change and evolve.
6. These are all *social* laws, not merely reflections of biological or physical factors.

THE AGE OF DISCOVERY

In the fifteenth century, a series of important developments opened the way for large additions to man's knowledge of man. A successful printing press was developed (1446); knowledge of paper was brought to Western Europe by the Arabs; and the fall of Constantinople (1453) brought a migration of Aristotelian scholars into Western Europe. All these developments had a catalytic effect on scholarship in the West.

Also, by the end of the fifteenth century, Portuguese, Spanish, and other seagoers had ventured far into hitherto unknown oceans, reaching the New World. There began a rapid accumulation of new knowledge about the peoples of the world—the Red Indians of America, island peoples of the South Seas, seal-and-caribou-hunting peoples of Greenland, the richly varied populations of India and southeast Asia, and the large populations of Negroes south of the Sahara desert barrier.

Theologically derived doctrines had divided all of mankind into descendants of Shem, Ham, and Japhet, all descended from Adam. The newly discovered varieties of peoples seemed not to fit very well into these categories. The first Spaniards active in exploring (and plundering) the New World claimed that the American Indians were not descendants of Adam, hence were outside the grace of God; this supposedly justified the cruelties carried out by the conquistadors. In 1512 the Pope declared that the American Indians were, indeed, descendants of Adam, hence entitled to be treated according to the same moral principles as Europeans. Explorers and exploiters continued to treat the "natives" as fair game, but individual Catholic missionaries often worked hard to protect the human rights of the Indians. Meanwhile, many scholars in Europe, including Paracelsus and Giordano Bruno, continued to maintain that

Ethiopians, South Sea Islanders, and other such physically "diferent" peoples were not the same species as Europeans.

Richard Hakluyt's *Divers Voyages Touching the Discovery of America* (1582) is perhaps the most famous of the many collections of geographical and anthropological information that began to be available to scholars of the sixteenth, seventeenth and eighteenth centuries. Other well-known works include the *Historia de Gentibus Septentrionalis* ("History of the People of the North") by Claus Magnus (1555), the mammoth seventy-three volume collection of *Jesuit Relations* gathered by missionaries in the New World between 1610 and 1791, Captain Cook's *Voyages* (1770's and 1780's), P. S. Pallas' account of his Russian journey (1771-76), and D. Crantz's *History of Greenland* (1767).

Ethnographic data from these volumes began to appear in the arguments of the Enlightenment philosophers. John Locke quoted from the *Jesuit Relations* in discussing his "social contract," and J. J. Rousseau introduced the idea of the "noble savage" into philosophical speculation, using the Carib Indians of Venezuela for his model.

THE RISE OF ANTHROPOLOGY

Those same philosophers of the Enlightenment had developed the ideas of progress and evolution that came to be the central focus of nineteenth-century anthropological theory, and many bits and pieces of anthropological ideas date back to those earlier centuries. But the story of human biological and cultural development began to take on a recognizable pattern only in the nineteenth century. Before that time, not only was descriptive information lacking, but obstacles of theological dogma had to be overcome as well.

Up to the beginning of the nineteenth century, many or most scholars dealing with human cultural diversity and history had accepted the age of the earth as pronounced by Archbishop Ussher in 1650. The good Archbishop had calculated from a careful study of the scriptures that the world had been created by God just 4,004 years before the birth of Christ, to which the theologian Dr. Lightfoot had added the demonstration that "heaven and earth, center and circumference, were created together, in the same instant, and clouds full of water . . . [and that] this work took place and man was created by the Trinity on the twenty-third of October, 4004 B.C. at nine o'clock in the morning." [7]

In the 1830's and 1840's, however, the French Abbe Boucher de Perthes discovered numbers of stone tools in the gravels of the river Somme, near Paris, and he began to insist on the immense antiquity of these works of man. Great theological and scientific argument raged, especially in France and England, over the age of these archaeological materials. Other significant archaeological finds were made both in France and England, and as early as 1825 a rhinoceros tooth had been found with a flint weapon in Kent's Cavern in England, by the Rev. J. MacEnery. The rapid accumulation of evidence about the Stone Age of man seriously undermined the orthodox, Biblical chronology of human cultural history.

Another striking development in the accumulating evidence concerning man's antiquity took place in a little river valley near Dusseldorf, in Germany. There, in 1857, were found portions of a human skeleton with features very different from those of modern man. The skull was massive, somewhat flattened on top, with extremely heavy brow ridges. The German doctor who first wrote about these human fossil remains described them as belonging to a "barbarous and savage race . . . the most ancient memorial of the early inhabitants of Europe." [8] This immensely important fossil had been found in the valley of the Neander River, hence its name— Neandertal Man.

By 1859, the year of publication of Darwin's *The Origin of Species*, leading scientists of Western Europe were ready to accept the theory that earth and man are very old; that the relative age of rocks, soil, and human artifacts can be read from their positions in the layers, or strata, laid down on the surface of the earth following known geological principles; and that the stone tools and skeletal remains from various sites in England, France, and elsewhere are evidence of the beginnings of human biological and cultural history dating from hundreds of thousands of years ago. Darwin's famous theory of natural selection provided a way of explaining man's relation to his natural world, and for understanding the relationship of Neandertal Man (and other such fossils) to modern *Homo sapiens*. Some scientists were quick to apply the basic principles of evolution to the nonbiological cultural materials as well.

---

[7] From *Man and His Gods*, p. 324, by Homer W. Smith. Copyright 1953 by Homer W. Smith. Reprinted by permission of Little, Brown and Company.
[8] T. K. Penniman, *A Hundred Years of Anthropology* (2nd ed., revised; London: Gerald Duckworth and Co., Ltd., 1952), p. 68.

EARLY APPLIED ANTHROPOLOGY

In Tasmania, where thousands were hunted down like beasts and shot, by 1835 only 203 aboriginals were left, the pitiful remnant of thousands. The last pure-blooded Tasmanian died in 1861. On the continent they did not fare much better. [Australian] Sheepherders, in order to clear the grazing-grounds more rapidly, offered them, in apparent friendliness, cakes of flour dosed with arsenic, and thus poisoned off black humanity like ground squirrels. Other ingenious native-exterminators poisoned the waterholes.[9]

The slaughter of aborigines, along with the vast inhumanity of the slave trade, aroused the consciences of many humanitarians in England and on the Continent. In 1837 the Aborigines Protection Society was founded in London, and a year later, with similar humane intentions, the Ethnological Society in Paris. The *Journal of the Ethnological Society* of London, in 1856, carried this statement:

> Ethnology is now generally recognized as having the strongest claims in our attention, not merely as it tends to gratify the curiosity of those who love to look into Nature's works, but also as being of great practical importance, especially in this country, whose numerous colonies and extensive commerce bring it into contact with so many varieties of the human species differing in their physical and moral qualities both from each other and from ourselves.[10]

The study of anthropology developed, therefore, from a fusion of theoretical and practical interests. On the one hand was the scholarly curiosity concerning the Stone Age, the rise of ancient civilizations, and the "strange and exotic" customs of diverse living peoples. At the same time, many of the early anthropologists were imbued with the conviction that knowledge of human cultures would bring immediate practical advantages to men—in the reduction of human cruelty, misery, and ignorance.

THE DOCTRINE OF CULTURAL EVOLUTION

Although anthropological theories of the evolution of culture were given a strong boost by the publication of Darwin's *The Origin of Species*, we should understand that the concepts of cul-

---

[9] H. R. Hays, *From Ape to Angel* (New York: Alfred A. Knopf, Inc., 1958), p. 85.
[10] Pp. 294–97.

tural evolution that dominated anthropological thinking in the nineteenth century were not directly an outgrowth of Darwinian ideas. The philosophers of the Enlightenment—especially Turgot and Condorcet—are principal sources for many of the ideas that composed the theory of cultural evolution. They held that the history of humans can be described as progress (betterment) from simple beginnings to our complex civilization. They set forth supposed stages through which human culture had progressed, starting with the creation, the fall, and the flood, followed by man's organization into small groups of hunters and gatherers, then the development of pastoralism, the inventions of agriculture and the idea of private property, the growth of villages, division of labor, and thence to modern civilization.

Lewis Henry Morgan

L. H. Morgan (1818-1881) is considered to be the founding father of American anthropology. Morgan was born in upstate New York, where he studied law at Union College in Schenectady, and then settled down to law practice, business, politics, and anthropological study in Rochester. As a young man, Morgan had founded the Order of the Gordian Knot at Aurora, organized around ideas of Greek mythology, secret rites, sacred paraphernalia, and other similar trappings. Somewhat later, the society was reorganized around American Indian ritual and mythology, as the Grand Order of the Iroquois. In collecting information about the Iroquois for these social activities, Morgan became interested in the Iroquois themselves and began to gather materials for more serious purposes. Soon he was deeply involved in trying to help the Iroquois against unscrupulous land-grabbers, meanwhile continuing his ethnographic notes. His *League of the Iroquois* (1851), the first fairly comprehensive monograph on a North American Indian tribe, resulted from these efforts.

In working with the Iroquois, Morgan had discovered some rather "peculiar" things about the kinship terms these people used in referring to their various relatives. An Iroquois individual called his mother's sister by the same word as he used in referring to his mother. Also, the father's brother—indeed quite a number of other male paternal relatives—were called by the same word as that used for one's father. Furthermore, the whole of Iroquois society was organized into matrilineal clans (kinship groups claiming descent through females only); and when a couple married they generally

TABLE 1
Morgan's Stages of Evolution

(Read from bottom up)

Stages	Cultural Example	Differentiating Characteristics
Civilization	Europeans, Americans	begins after the alphabet was invented
Higher Barbarism	Greeks of ancient time	begins with use of iron
Middle Barbarism	Zuni, Hopi Indians	begins with domestication of animals and plants
Lower Barbarism	Iroquois Indians	begins with invention of pottery
Higher Savagery	Polynesians	begins with use of bow and arrow
Middle Savagery	Australian aborigines	begins with fish diet, use of fire and speech
Lower Savagery	no known examples	before fire and speech were invented

settled down with the bride's kin rather than joining the man's kin group or establishing a household of their own.

Morgan searched for an explanation of the Iroquois patterns of kinship terminology, and thought he found it in the idea of "survivals." That is, if all human societies (including the Iroquois) had passed through an evolutionary stage of "group marriage"— the union of several men with several women, the Iroquois called several people "mother" and numbers of older males "father" as a relic from that bygone stage of society.

Morgan collected information on kinship systems from many parts of the world and wove them into the fabric of Enlightenment theorizing about human progress, adding many innovations of his own. Table 1 shows the main stages of human cultural evolution from Morgan's most famous book, *Ancient Society*.[11]

The basic philosophical premises of Morgan's evolutionary system are similar to the ideas underlying the writings of most other well-known anthropologists of the nineteenth century. They assumed

[11] New York: Holt, Rinehart & Winston, Inc., 1877.

that all men are rational beings who strive to improve themselves. They assumed that mankind is part of nature, hence developing in accordance with natural laws. These laws of the universe were considered to be unchanging through time. In general, they felt that evolution proceeds from simple to complex, from unorganized to organized, and, especially, that this development is directly associated with betterment—that evolution is simultaneously progress, the march toward human perfection.

In 1879, Morgan was elected president of the American Association for the Advancement of Science, and in the same year he was offered the directorship of the newly created Bureau of American Ethnology. Morgan was ill, however, and urged his friend, Colonel John Wesley Powell, to take that important position. Morgan was the acknowledged leader of American anthropology when he died in 1881.

Edward B. Tylor

Edward B. Tylor was Morgan's English counterpart. In his most important book, *Primitive Culture* (1871), he elaborated his version of the story of evolution with special concentration on religion. He believed that the earliest primitive religion had been "animism"—the belief that persons, animals, and even trees and stones have indwelling spirits or souls. The origin of this belief and hence the origin of religion, Tylor theorized, is to be found in man's seeking rationally to explain what happens in dreaming and death.

During the nineteenth century, theologians argued, following Biblical interpretation, that man had fallen from grace and that primitive peoples had degenerated the furthest from the original high culture of paradise. Tylor and the evolutionists claimed, on the other hand, that primitive peoples like the Australians are examples of the rude beginnings of all mankind and that everywhere there is progress from savagery toward civilization, though some peoples (possibly due to isolation and other factors) have not progressed as far as others in this evolution.

Although he held no university degree, Tylor became the foremost anthropologist in England and was appointed the first Professor of Anthropology at Oxford (1896). He quite accurately predicted that the new science would develop "from a derided byway of truth to a time when its help and decisions are sought for by governments."

Other nineteenth-century scholars contributed important ideas to the growing science. In England, Sir John Lubbock coined the now familiar terms *palaeolithic* and *neolithic* in the course of his studies of prehistory; Sir Henry Maine, in his *Ancient Law* (1861), laid the foundations for the comparative study of legal systems; later, Sir James G. Frazer collected and organized an amazing mass of information on magic and religion, widely known in the several editions of his *Golden Bough*. A Swiss jurist, J. J. Bachofen, published a richly documented argument for an early stage of matrilineality in human culture history (*Das Mutterrecht,* 1861). And in Germany, the tireless traveler and writer, Adolph Bastian, is honored as the founder of the Royal Ethnological Museum in Berlin and co-founder of the Berlin Society for Anthropology, Ethnology, and Prehistory.

REACTION TO EVOLUTION

As the nineteenth century neared its close, some anthropologists began to have serious doubts about Morgan's and Tylor's theories of cultural evolution. These anti-evolutionist scholars doubted that all human societies pass through the same stages. They denied that human history always has represented progress, and they advanced the idea that human culture history is best understood as the result of complex diffusion of cultural elements among human groups.

The most extreme anti-evolutionists were the Englishmen, W. J. Perry and Sir Grafton Elliot Smith, who claimed that peoples of the world are so unimaginative that practically all cultural development must have been invented in one place—Egypt—and diffused from there throughout the world. The metallurgy, agriculture, architecture, complex society, religious practices, and other cultural attainments of Maya, Aztec, and Inca civilizations, for example, they explained as inventions borrowed from the center of all things —Egypt.

Austrian anthropologists also developed an anti-evolutionist school of thought in the beginning of the twentieth century, somewhat less extreme than the Egypt-centered theories. Fritz Graebner and Peter Wilhelm Schmidt, leaders of the "Vienna school," believed that original human culture developed somewhere in Asia, and from this *Urkultur* there developed several distinct *Kulturkriese* ("culture complexes") in different environments. Great migrations of peoples carried these ancient *Kulturkreise* into widely separated parts of the globe. For example, the *exogamous matrilineal kulturkreise*, which has hoe-agriculture, plank boats, moon mythology, rectangular houses with gabled roofs, and men's secret societies, was supposedly carried to both the New Guinea area and to Africa. The *Kulturkreise* anthropologists have been heavily criticized for weaknesses of theory, but they frequently are applauded for their extensive field work.

In American anthropology, one single individual stands out as the man who "overthrew" cultural evolutionist theories. The man was Franz Boas. Boas was educated in Germany, taking his degree in geography and physics. His professors had guided him to a firm empiricism, insisting that facts come first and theory later. During geographical field work in Baffinland (1883-84), he realized that his main interests tended toward the study of people instead of climate and physical landscape, so he became an anthropologist, ultimately taking a joint position at Columbia University and the American Museum of Natural History (1895). Columbia University quickly became a focal point of anthropological activity, as growing numbers of Boasian students began extensive field studies among American Indians. Clark Wissler, A. L. Kroeber, Robert Lowie, Margaret Mead, Ruth Benedict, and Melville Herskovits are among the better known of Boas' students.

It is hard for us to realize that in the 1890's—a relatively few years ago—there were still free bands of Indians, threatened but not yet crushed by the waves of covered wagoners, gold miners, railroad workers, army troops and other settlers of the American West. To Boas and his students, every day spent in one's library theorizing about evolution, culture history, and other vague, abstract ideas, meant one day's loss of priceless, irretrievable ethnographic data. So they went out in the summers and at every other conceivable opportunity, with small amounts of expense money provided by the Museum, to collect information and cultural artifacts from the Dakota, Cheyenne, Blackfoot, Crow, Apache, and other groups that only a few years previously had hunted buffalo, raided each other's horse herds, and fought American army units (and one another) in the Great Plains. Boas himself carried out extensive field work among the Kwakiutl and other tribes of the British Columbia seacoast.

From the accumulating masses of ethnographic data on American Indians, Boas and his followers shaped a strongly anti-evolutionary theory. They denounced Morgan's stages as figments of imagination, unsupported by evidence. The complexities of ethnographic information do not fit into neat stages, they claimed. For example, several Indian tribes of the Great Plains had given up settled agricultural life in favor of nomadic buffalo-hunting—

strictly the reverse of the Morgan-Tylor evolutionary sequences. They saw the history of man as a sort of "tree of culture," with fantastically complex branching, intertwining, and budding off—each branch representing a uniquely different cultural complex, to be understood in terms of its own unique history rather than compared to cultural complexes in other world regions in some grand scheme of "stages of evolution." Some of the differences between this new "culture historical" and the evolutionary perspective on human culture can be seen in Figure 1.

Other points at which this new "American school" of anthropology differed with the evolutionists include:

Denial of the idea that development could be equated with progress or betterment.

Refusal to consider widely separated cultures as representatives of broad "culture types," such as the all-embracing category, "savagery."

Organization of the world of ethnographic data into "culture areas," each thought to be unique in culture history, with a resulting distinctive array of culture elements, or traits.

The differences between evolutionist and anti-evolutionist views have often obscured certain fundamental agreements. Both emphasized the rationality and humanity of primitive peoples; they were in thorough agreement that cultural differences are due to culture history and not biological inequalities; and both schools of thought were fundamentally opposed to the theological view that primitive peoples have "degenerated" from a state of original paradise. Evolutionists and anti-evolutionists alike constructed their theories by interrelating evidence from human biology, archaeology, study of languages, and ethnography.

PSYCHOLOGICAL AND CONFIGURATIONAL STUDIES

It is always the individual that really thinks and acts and dreams and revolts.[12]

This credo was written by Edward Sapir, one of Boas' most brilliant students, in reaction to what he felt to be the depersonalization inherent in the study of culture complexes, diffusion of

---

[12] Edward Sapir, "Do We Need a Superorganic?" *American Anthropologist,* XIX (1917), 441–47.

The Tree of Culture

American Historical School

Unilinear Evolution
(Morgan, Tylor, et al.)

Civilization

Barbarism

Savagery

Modern Western Civilization

Iroquois

Polynesians

Pueblo Indians

Australian Aborigines

Figure 1. Two Views of Cultural History.

customs, and reconstruction of culture history. Human beings had come to be looked on as passive "culture carriers" without individual significance for the study of anthropology. In a series of papers and seminars, Sapir and a few other American anthropologists began in the 1920's and 30's to work toward an inclusion of psychological study in anthropology. One of Sapir's articles was aptly entitled, "Why Cultural Anthropology Needs the Psychiatrist."

Another of Boas' students, Margaret Mead, became interested in psychiatry and the relationships of personality and culture; for her first major field work, she set out to study psychological problems of adolescents among the Samoans. *Coming of Age in Samoa* (1928) is a pioneer effort in this new anthropological direction.

In a series of seminars during the 1930's at Columbia University, Ralph Linton (anthropologist) and Abram Kardiner (psychiatrist) collaborated in producing a new approach to psychologically-oriented anthropology. Kardiner and Linton formulated the idea of "basic personality" as a unifying concept for understanding man and culture. The "basic personality" of a given people is that pattern of psychological characteristics common to all or most of the members of the society brought about by similarities in child training practices. The basic personality of a society, once established, is reflected in many areas of custom—particularly in religious beliefs and practices, art, mythology, and popular fantasies.

Cora DuBois applied this general frame of theory in her colorful study of *The People of Alor* (1944). Among the Alorese, located on one of the easternmost islands of Indonesia, Dr. DuBois gathered information about child training and individual dreams, biographies of individuals, as well as data about economic, social, and ritual-cultural patterns. She also obtained responses to Rorschach (ink-blot) tests and other psychological materials. Her findings suggest that Alorese children suffer great anxieties about their feeding and care, leading to food-anxieties and other important personality characteristics among the adults. These elements of personality are in turn explanations for themes about food, hunger, and other anxieties in their religious rituals, folk tales, and individual dreams.

Culture-and-personality studies developed rapidly in the 1940's, and many anthropologists began to use personality tests in the course of field work among the American Indians, peoples of the South Sea Islands, and other parts of the world. Interest also developed concerning mental illness and types of "abnormality" in primitive societies. All of these studies express a strong, continuing interrelationship between anthropological and psychological theories of human behavior.

Another reaction to the piecemeal cataloguing of customs and complexes developed into what have been called "configurational studies." Ruth Benedict's *Patterns of Culture* (1934) is the best-known expression of this trend. Taking the Pueblo Indians of the Southwest, the Kwakiutl of British Columbia, and the Dobu of the South Pacific for her main examples, she attempted to demonstrate that each culture is not just a random collection of customs haphazardly "borrowed" or diffused from surrounding cultures. Each culture, she maintained, is organized around some central configuration of ideas. Among the Pueblos it is an "Apollonian" moderation and restraint in all things, adherence to the golden mean; Kwakiutl culture, on the other hand, is supposedly pervaded by individualistic, megalomaniacal competition for prestige and honor; while Dobuan culture is characterized by a paranoid, sorcery-ridden hostility of all against all. In each case, the economy, kinship patterns, religious practices, and other major elements of custom are all thought to be shaped and interrelated by the one dominant motif.

Many anthropologists feel that Benedict's configurations were too simple and could only be maintained by ignoring much contrary evidence. M. E. Opler advanced the idea of "themes" of culture. Using Apache culture as an example, he suggested that a system of several elemental themes, rather than a single configuration, better expresses the organization of a given culture. Other anthropologists, particularly in postwar times, have developed the study of cultural values and postulates in similar attempts to describe the thematic interrelatedness of human cultural systems.

FUNCTIONALIST ANTHROPOLOGY

The main lines of anthropology in both America and Europe have come to be influenced increasingly by the so-called structural-functional school of social theory. Several writers in the nineteenth century, including Herbert Spencer, Fustel de Coulanges, and August Comte, developed theories of human social behavior that likened societies to organisms, in which the parts—the institutions, or custom complexes of the society—function to maintain the life of the society.

Following their example, Emile Durkheim, the French scholar, set forth a theory of the origins and functions of religion. He amassed evidence to show that in Australian totemic practices each social group, clan, or other kin group worships a particular totemic animal, or other natural phenomenon, and in so doing such groups are really worshipping themselves; the totemic animal or plant seems to be a symbol of the social group itself. Durkheim concluded:

> In a general way, it is unquestionable that a society has all that is necessary to arouse the sensation of the divine in minds, merely by the power that it has over them; for to its members it is what a god is to his worshippers . . . religious force is nothing other than the collective and anonymous force of the clan . . .[13]

His studies of other human institutions and customs also dwell heavily on the way these customs contribute to the maintenance of society.

Durkheim's writings strongly influenced A. R. Radcliffe-Brown, a British anthropologist who had done field work among the Andaman Islanders off the east coast of India. Radcliffe-Brown became a leading figure in British social anthropology during the period before and after World War II, and his influence is still strongly felt. He shares the limelight in functional studies with another famous anthropologist, Polish-born Bronislaw Malinowski.

Malinowski had done his doctoral work in mathematics and had also studied physics and chemistry. While on a rest from his studies, he read Frazer's *Golden Bough* and was inspired to study anthropology. After a period of study in London, he went to the Trobriand Islands, off the coast of New Guinea, and spent the entire duration of World War I (four years) engaged in research on the language, social organization, religion, economic practices, and nearly every other aspect of the Trobriand way of life. Very few field workers have so thoroughly immersed themselves in the daily lives of a people for purposes of anthropological study.

The Trobriand Islanders, like the Lycians described by Herodotus, are matrilineal in kinship organization, and Malinowski realized that they constituted a crucial test of Freud's Oedipus complex theory. According to Freud's view, all peoples everywhere

---

[13]*The Elementary Forms of the Religious Life*, trans. Joseph Ward Swain (New York: Collier Books, 1961), pp. 236 ff.

are supposed to experience the Oedipal problem: the management of aggression toward one's father because of sexual jealousies concerning one's mother, accompanied by suppressed sexual longing for the mother. Among the matrilineal Trobrianders, however, Malinowski found that a growing boy's hostilities are directed at his maternal uncle, because that uncle is the person who has authority over the boy and trains him for adult life. The Trobriand boy's father is a friendly, helpful person, and exercises little or no authority over his son. Also, Malinowski found that sexual guilt over forbidden desires involved not the mother, but the sister; thus the ethnographic data from the matrilineal Trobrianders suggested that sharp revision was needed in Freudian psychological theory.

As Malinowski wrote and published more of his Trobriand Islands materials, a new theoretical framework took shape. To him, cultural practices make up a tightly interrelated network, the whole of which is to be understood in terms of relationships to the psychobiological needs of individuals in society. While Durkheim and Radcliffe-Brown interpreted magic and religion as serving the needs of *societies* as organisms, Malinowski pointed to the way in which these practices and beliefs can be understood as responses to the needs of the *individual* human organism.

For example, Malinowski noted that the Trobriand Islanders (and their neighbors) do not use magic in seagoing operations that are safe and sound, near shore. For such ventures their canoe-building and sailing techniques are perfectly adequate. But when they must sail farther out, where sudden storms or other unforeseen events can overtake the sailor and render useless all knowledge, skills, and techniques—where a man's life is in the hands of powers beyond the reach of his "science"—there the individual experiences helpless anxiety. Magical acts are performances that function to relieve such anxiety.

The "functionalist school" of anthropology has thus developed two differing theoretical tendencies. Malinowskian functional interpretation often emphasizes the supposed needs of individuals, while followers of Durkheim and Radcliffe-Brown stress the supposed needs of a social system. Both types of functionalism developed a strong bias against historical studies, for they attempted analysis of a socio-cultural system operating at a given point in time. Functionalist theory has led to great improvements in field research, since analysis of the functional importance of particular customs and institutions often leads to more thorough and systematic gathering of information than does simple cataloguing of customs.

POSTWAR DEVELOPMENTS IN ANTHROPOLOGICAL THOUGHT

From the foregoing we see that, by the beginning of World War II, the Boasian "anti-evolutionist" school of anthropology had experienced sharp modifications. From a number of points of view the individual, the acting person and his psychological characteristics, has been reintroduced into general theorizing about the nature of human behavioral patterns. More and more, culture and society are both looked on as systems, functionally interwoven structures, rather than as simply agglomerations or lists of cultural customs and institutions.

A more sober appraisal of culture history led many anthropologists to admit that there were germs of truth, after all, in many of the ideas of Morgan and Tylor and other nineteenth-century "armchair theorists"; in fact, at least one anthropologist (Leslie White) has taken the position that Lewis Henry Morgan was a great thinker whose signal contributions to anthropology had been entirely, almost maliciously, misrepresented by the Boasians and other later anthropologists. White and his followers have built up a massive array of materials and arguments reinterpreting Morgan's evolutionist ideas in a new light, strongly colored by their "energy theory" of culture. In this view, cultural development is the result of changes in amounts of energy available to societies, influenced by the type of technology used to utilize the energy sources.

During World War II, anthropologists were called upon to make their special knowledge helpful to the U.S. and Allied cause. Anthropologists reshaped ethnographic information into manuals and handbooks about New Guinea, the peoples of Southeast Asia, survival in the jungle and desert, and how to win the affections of hostile natives. Other anthropologists studied the cultural characteristics of major nations—both enemy and ally—to provide information for military decisions as well as for handbooks on how to understand the British. Ruth Benedict's *Chrysanthemum and the*

Sword, concerning the Japanese national culture, is one of the best known of these wartime products.

When the war was over, anthropologists were called in as "trouble-shooters" in the administration of island communities in the South Pacific. They had the dual job of interpreting administrative policies to the natives and trying to explain native customs and reactions to administrators. Often the anthropological knowledge was helpful, but difficulties arose because of differences in points of view between administrator and anthropologist. Homer G. Barnett has described some of these problems in his book, *Anthropology and Administration.*

The Society for Applied Anthropology had been founded in 1941, and the pages of its journal, *Human Organization,* now carry a variety of articles concerning anthropological study of mental hospitals, community development programs in Latin America, and many other applied programs. India has been the scene of particularly intense activities, and anthropologists have found themselves coping with problems of introduction of new medical practices, new crops and agricultural techniques, and many other practical problems.

Other tendencies that mark current anthropological studies are:

Increased interest in study of complex modern societies, including community studies in Japan, Europe, Mexico, and inside the United States.

Increased co-operation with sociologists, psychologists, geographers, and scholars in related fields.

Increased interrelating of historical, functionalist, biological, psychological, and even evolutionist concepts into a unified theory of human behavior.

In this review of the history of anthropology it appears that one can roughly (and arbitrarily) divide the succession of recent events into (approximately) fifty-year periods: 1850 to 1900 marks the rise and decline of evolutionism; 1900 to 1945 may be regarded as the "Boasian" or "culture historical" period (Boas died in 1942); and the end of World War II marks the beginning of new developments in anthropology. We can only guess at the outlines of the anthropology that will characterize the final decades of the twentieth century.

Suggested Reading

*Hays, H. R. *From Ape to Angel: An Informal History of Social Anthropology*. New York: G. P. Putnam's Sons, 1964.

This well-illustrated book treats the reader to casual glimpses into the personal lives and research efforts of Morgan, Tylor, Boas, Frazer, and a long list of other eminent anthropologists.

*Kardiner, Abram, and Edward Preble. *They Studied Man*. Mentor Books edition; New York: New American Library of World Literature, Inc., 1963.

These authors discuss the lives and works of a selected group of scholars, working up from Morgan and Tylor to Sigmund Freud and Abram Kardiner in order to highlight the strong interrelations that have grown up between psychoanalysis and anthropology.

Advanced Reading

Bunzel, Ruth, and Margaret Mead. *The Golden Age of American Anthropology*. New York: George Braziller, Inc., 1960.

This is a collection of colorful writings from the early days of anthropology, mainly illustrating nineteenth- and early twentieth-century ethnographic reporting on the American Indians.

Penniman, T. K. *One Hundred Years of Anthropology* (2nd ed.). London: Gerald Duckworth and Co., Ltd., 1952.

The British have a somewhat different view of the definition and scope of anthropology, and this book is a useful supplement to our version of the history of anthropology.

---

* Paperback.

chapter three

Methods of Anthropological Research

The field of anthropology may be looked on as a "subculture," with its own social organization, customs, values, and ways of doing things. In this chapter we shall examine briefly the "customs" and procedures that anthropologists employ in the search for information about the nature of man.

Field work is undoubtedly the favorite activity of anthropologists, for research in all the subfields of anthropology is frequently pursued in out-of-the-way places, distant lands—in Africa, the Arctic, or the South Pacific. An anthropologist's first field trip—particularly if it deals with a primitive society, far from cities and civilization—is regarded as an initiation rite after which he is "never the same again." It can truthfully be said that those few anthropologists who have concentrated on library research and avoided the risks and rigors of field work are looked down on by the rest of the profession.

The romantic aura around field work sometimes obscures the fact that the anthropologist collects information in the field for later painstaking work at home—in the laboratory and the library. For every month spent in Africa, the South Seas, or the jungles of New Guinea, the anthropologist usually spends many months analyzing and writing up his findings.

ARCHAEOLOGY

Nearly everyone who has watched adventure shows on television or has read one of the many accounts of finding lost cities or ancient treasures has some ideas about the methods of archaeological research. The idea of digging recurs over and over in our mental image of the archaeologist, and the field project of an archaeologist is often referred to as a "dig."

What is not generally known, however, is the highly developed pattern of techniques the archaeologist employs in accomplishing his field-work objectives.

1. Meticulous care is taken that excavated materials are not damaged in the process of digging.

2. The position and context of every object excavated is recorded by a combination of drawings, notes, and photographs so that the archaeologist can later establish with great accuracy which items found in an excavation belong together in a particular complex of materials for a particular time period, as represented, for example, in the levels of deposited materials—the stratigraphy— of a given site.

3. All significant associated items are collected and recorded: soil samples, remains of animal and vegetable materials, types of rocks and other geological specimens, and all kinds of other materials associated with the monuments, buildings, burial goods, jewels, artwork, stone tools, weapons, or other human handiwork that the archaeologist uncovers.

Well-financed amateur archaeologists who report amazing finds of "lost cities," "fantastic works of art," and "untranslated inscriptions" are often found to be despoilers of archaeological materials because they do *not* attend carefully to the major requirements of mapping and recording mentioned above. When an archaeological find is dug up carelessly, there is usually no way to go about establishing the time sequences of materials, the relationships of various objects to one another, and other information crucial to scientific study. In a way, the archaeologist is something like a detective, for the clues he searches for are often extremely subtle.

In order to carry out the preserving of data and materials, the archaeologist often must bring a portable laboratory to his field-work location. Having set up his equipment at an archaeological site (often the selection of the site itself is the result of months of painstaking exploration and surveying), the archaeologist maps out the main outlines within which he will work. The places to be excavated are divided into carefully measured tracts—perhaps four-foot squares, for example, and each digger goes to work in a particular tract, exercising great care not to damage any materials he unearths. When the archaeologist finds any significant object—a tool, a skeleton, a scrap of a work of art—he uncovers it very slowly, sometimes using such fine tools as dental picks, toothbrushes, and small paint brushes in order to avoid damaging delicate materials. Without special training in these techniques, a digger would break up and ruin many of the objects discovered.

When the archaeologist has his thousands and thousands of items excavated, marked, recorded, classified, and shipped safely back to his home laboratory, the field-work stage of his research is over and the hard work of scientific analysis begins in earnest. (Once again, the mark of the *amateur* archaeologist is that he often contents himself with the exhilaration of exhibition and description of what he found in the field work, without going into the hard work of analysis that would convert his results into useful scientific knowledge.)

Dating Archaeological Remains

A major methodological problem that faces the archaeologist is the matter of chronology—establishing time periods and sequences for materials that have no written evidence of dates attached to them. Archaeological publications are full of time charts of cultural materials—put together from pieces of information gleaned from hundreds of different excavations. Some of the major methods of establishing sequences and dates for archaeological materials include:

Stratigraphic evidence. If an archaeological site is relatively undisturbed, it often can be assumed that materials found close to the surface are newer or younger than materials found deep in the ground.

Association with plant and animal remains. For example, flint handaxes found with the bones of long-extinct types of elephants, mammoths, and other animals, are among the important chronological clues for early man in Western Europe. Similarly, the bones of extinct forms of camels, horses, and bison found with Indian artifacts help to establish relative ages of some North American archaeological remains.

Pollen analysis. Pollen grains found in association with archaeological finds may tell the archaeologist what kinds of plants grew in the area at the time the materials were left on the ground. Particular combinations of plants may have been characteristic of the area at only certain time periods in the past.

Dendrochronology (tree-ring dating). Annual tree-rings display variable patterns of spacing, depending on the wetness or dryness of particular years. Each sequence of years forms a unique pattern of rings. Many of the rich archaeological remains in Arizona and New Mexico have been dated by systematic tree-ring analysis of the timbers found in the sites.

Calendar dating. Some advanced civilizations, such as that of the Maya in Middle America and the Egyptian and Sumerian in the Old World, had calendrical systems, and dates of some archaeological materials may be interpolated from carved inscriptions. The big problem for the archaeologist is often the deciphering and analysis of the calendrical systems.

Cross-dating from other cultural materials. Sometimes archaeological sites in Europe have coins included in them for which nearly exact dates are obtainable. This establishes that the site *cannot be older* than those dated coins, but it may be younger.

Association with extinct shorelines and other geological features. In northern Europe, where the Finnish and Scandinavian lands continue to rise out of the sea at a relatively constant rate, archaeological finds that were originally at the seashore, or at the edge of a lake, can be dated by calculation of the approximate number of hundreds of years it has taken for that shoreline to rise so far from the water. A striking case of this sort is a series of rock carvings on a cliff in northern Norway which could only have been reached by boat. Since the carvings are now a number of feet above sea level, it is estimated that the works of art are several thousands of years old.

Radiological dating. Radiocarbon dating is one of the most striking scientific developments affecting archaeological work in recent years. This method depends on the fact that plants and animals contain a fixed amount of a radioactive isotope of carbon, called C_{14}, which deteriorates after death at a constant rate, leaving ordinary carbon (C_{12}).

By measuring the amount of C_{14} radioactivity remaining in a particular specimen, archaeologists can obtain an estimated date for that specimen and the materials associated with it. This method of dating puts the entire problem of archaeological dating on a much firmer footing. Gathering the materials (charcoal, wood, and plant fibers are preferred) for radiocarbon analysis requires great care by the archaeologist to insure that the materials are not contaminated by contact with other things that would affect the C_{14} count of the sample.

Since most of the measurable radioactive carbon is gone from a given sample after about 45,000 years, this method of dating is not useful for remains older than that figure. Archaeologists hope very much that physicists will discover other kinds of radioactive materials for accurate dating of objects in the range of 50,000 to 1,000,000 years old.

The dating of materials occupies an important place in our discussion because so much archaeological analysis depends on first establishing the ages of various sites and materials relative to one another. When the archaeologist has established some dates for his materials, his task is only begun, however. The modern archaeologist is interested in inferring general social and cultural facts from the material objects left in the ground. For example, if he excavates a small village and finds that all the house remains are alike except for one that is much larger, richer, and better furnished, he may be led to infer that the larger house represents the dwelling of a chief. On the other hand, if the unusual house floor has numbers of ritual objects in it, it may be suggested that the special occupant was a religious leader. Complex inferences from archaeological remains allow the archaeologist to speak of growth of empires, overthrow of dynasties, development of a middle class, spread of new religions, increasing craft specialization, victories and defeats in warfare, and other important social events. It is easy to see, then, why the archaeologist can make a significant contribution to history, as well as to other fields of study.

PHYSICAL ANTHROPOLOGY

"Digging up old skeletons" is the usual stereotype of field work in physical anthropology, and this is still an important part of that branch of study. One culture hero among physical anthropologists, Dr. L. S. B. Leakey, has spent a large portion of his adult life in searching for human fossil remains in East Africa. His recent finds of human remains dating possibly from nearly two million years ago are the fruits of many years of field work. Much of the field work of the physical anthropologist takes the same patterns, digging for and dating remains, that were described for the archaeologist. In fact, they often work together. The main difference between the two areas of study is that the archaeologist seeks information concerning man's culture history, while the physical anthropologist searches for evidence of man's biological evolution.

Physical anthropologists also carry out field research on living human communities. In the past this activity often consisted of obtaining measurements of peoples' height, weight, eye color, hair texture and color, and—most important of all—the cephalic index, or skull measurement. The cephalic index, obtained by dividing the width of the skull by its length, was formerly thought to be a very important clue to relationships among the different populations, or "races" of people. More recent investigations have shown, however, that the supposedly fixed and reliable cephalic index can be strongly affected by environment. Some populations that were thought to be long-headed have in some mysterious way become more round-headed, forcing abandonment of that means of "racial" classification.

New, revolutionary developments in physical anthropology have produced greatly refined methods of measurement and observation of human physical types. Increasingly, the physical anthropologists are concerned with *internal* characteristics of the human body—components of the blood and other body fluids, measures of body fat (obtained by examining skin folds and through X rays), blood pressures, growth rates, and many other complex characteristics of people. Analysis of blood types has been particularly important in recent years, for it has been found that the A-B-O blood types, and the other, lesser-known components of blood, are excellent clues to genetic inheritance.

LINGUISTICS

Nineteenth-century linguists had very little equipment to aid them in field work. Having arrived in the community in which he intended to study a particular language, the linguist located an informant (someone willing and able to speak to the linguist in the local tongue) and asked him to say particular words and sentences. The linguist simply relied on his own ears to pick up the sounds of the language, which he transcribed into his notebooks in the form of phonetic markings—the linguists' own special cross-cultural alphabet. Very often, of course, the linguist also needed an interpreter to help him, unless his informants were bilingual.

The linguist frequently collects his information on language in the form of stories—folk tales, myths, and so on, so that the professional linguist may be a collector of folklore as well.

Thomas Alva Edison's phonograph (patented in 1877) produced a major revolution in the field methods of linguists. The year after the phonograph was available to the public, the anthropologist J. W. Fewkes used one to collect forty cylinders of sample vocabularies, folklore texts, conversations, and other materials from the Passamaquoddy Indians in Maine. For the first time, the sounds of

the native speaker—his own intonations and speech patterns—
could be stored away to be played back later as the linguist analyzed
his data.

The nineteenth-century linguist generally analyzed languages
by analogy with the categories of Latin, the language of scholars.
Description of a previously unstudied language involved the search
for nouns, adjectives, prepositions, prefixes, suffixes, and other
familiar elements of grammar. It was Franz Boas and his students
who broke away from the narrow view of Latin grammatical categories and concentrated on description of American Indian languages in terms of their own "natural" grammatical elements.

Linguists have found that each language is a self-contained and
unique system for categorizing and talking about experience; some
languages do not even have words in the way we ordinarily think
of the word *word*. The Eskimo language, for example, expresses
ideas such as "The man stood on the high hill" in complex clusters
of "idea particles" or morphemes, which cannot be separated out
into six or seven words, as in the English sentence, but rather are
all stuck together into a single "word-sentence."

Although linguists try to describe individual languages in terms
of their own intrinsic patterns of grammar and sounds, they make
systematic comparisons among languages, searching for "families
of languages" descended from common ancestors. As mentioned
earlier, the discovery that most of the languages in Europe are
all descended from a common ancestral proto-Indo-European
language was one of the great revolutionary developments of
linguistics. Related languages are discovered by systematic comparison of their vocabularies for sound-and-meaning correspond-
ences. For example, if *hound* in English refers to a kind of dog, and
hund in German also refers to man's best friend, then it is probable
that both words are derived from a common ancestral form. Systematic comparison of large numbers of such English-German word
pairs provides the evidence that the two languages are related. The
linguist's comparative method becomes quite complicated by the
fact that all languages change in pronunciation and grammar over
the years and centuries. The similarities between German and
English are relatively easy to spot, but it is harder to understand
how, for example, the Russian word pronounced *adyin* is related to
our English word *one*.

The research methods of the linguist, like those of other anthropologists, have been greatly assisted by modern mechanical devices
such as magnetic recorders, sound spectrographs, and electronic

computers, but none of these machines make any less complex the painstaking analysis that the researcher must carry out with his own brain, eyes, and hands.

THE METHODS OF SOCIAL ANTHROPOLOGY

The cultural (social) anthropologist gathers his raw materials by means of field work in primitive or not-so-primitive communities, where he usually lives for several months. (Many current field studies last over a year.) He attempts to observe as much as possible of the ways of life of the people he is studying. There are many recent innovations in field-work techniques, but the old and the new methods of field work that the anthropologist uses are variations around two major procedures: 1) interviewing of informants, and 2) participant observation.

Like the linguist, the social anthropologist seeks out reliable, knowledgeable informants—those people in the community who know the most about the life of the community, and are the most willing to tell what they know. In some communities nearly everyone is willing to tell a lot about the local way of life; in other places the anthropologist must work hard to establish enough trust so that even one or two people will consent to give extensive information. Again, like the linguist, the anthropologist must often hire an interpreter, unless he has learned the local language beforehand. Nowadays, of course, in increasing numbers of societies there are highly capable bilinguals whose second language is English or French or Spanish. But most anthropologists seek to learn the local language during their field-work period—even if field work is possible in the anthropologist's own language. The reasons for the anthropologist's interest in language are threefold: 1) most people in primitive and folk communities feel increasing closeness and trust toward those outsiders who make an attempt to learn their language; 2) the anthropologist who does not speak the local language misses much information because he does not understand conversations going on around him; 3) frequently the social meanings of particular elements of human behavior are poorly expressed in translated form, and the anthropologist cannot get an adequate understanding of them until he has full descriptions in the native tongue.

The experiences of anthropologists and others have taught us over the years that even in a small community any one informant does not know all about life in that community, nor is he always accurate in telling what he knows. Any informant in a small town probably knows how many policemen and doctors there are. Most informants know which local stores have what commodities. But few informants can be uniformly reliable in matters of what towns-people eat for supper, what they think about outsiders, where people go for medical care, and other complex human affairs. Therefore, the anthropologist tries to locate and use the services of a number of different informants who occupy diverse positions in the local community. He tries to interview individuals from different family groups, different neighborhoods, different social classes, and other major sub-units of the local society. The information given by these various persons can be cross-checked for accuracy. Often the upper-class members of a village are not well informed on the details of behavior of lower-class individuals, and vice versa.

Even the best informants, cross-checked against one another, provide the anthropologist with a very distilled, inadequate picture of life in a society. A native might be completely unconscious of, or take for granted, and thus not mention, aspects of his culture that would have great significance to the outside observer. Much of the richness of information the anthropologist wants from the tribe or village or band that he is studying can be obtained only by "participant observation"—the participation by the anthropologist in the activities themselves. The anthropologist hopes to be so accepted in the regular life of the community that he can be present and take part in hunting activities, planting of crops, religious ceremonies, initiation rites, weddings and wakes, as well as the day-to-day routines of social interaction—visiting, gossiping, games, and other recreation in the community.

As participant observer the anthropologist tries to accomplish several major objectives. First, he hopes that by being involved rather extensively in the local life, he can gain the respect and trust of the local people, so that they will feel confidence in him and willingly reveal to him aspects of their private lives. Second, participation is often the best way to see the complex details of human behavior. A Pueblo rainmaking ceremony, for example, cannot be fully described by an informant, however eloquent he may be. It has to be seen by the anthropologist for himself. Having seen the ceremony, he can then ask intelligent questions about it, for fuller understanding. Third, the anthropologist often finds that the *emotional* meaning of a particular human activity does not become clear to him until he has experienced the activity himself. The anthropologist, thus, is an investigator who wants to find out how it "feels" to take part in an arduous hunting expedition, to dance all night in a harvest festival, or to sit in a darkened room watching and listening to the performance of a gifted "shaman" or medicine man as he cures a sick person.

In this writer's field work among Lappish people in northeastern Finland, the complexities, the excitement, and the subtle interaction of men and animals in the reindeer roundup came clear only after he had actually worked in the corral trying to rope some of the elusive animals.

THE PATTERNING OF BEHAVIOR

Anthropologists frequently point out that the ways of life of a given people contain many customs or patterns of behavior that are highly predictable, highly regular, so that no statistical count is necessary to substantiate the generalizations made by the anthropologist. Such highly regular patterning of behavior is most clearly seen in language. We do not need to study a large sample of informants in order to find out what the past tense of the verb *run* is supposed to be. The logic of patterning (the rules) of language is such that nearly all English speakers agree on the use of the term *ran* as the past tense. In simple societies, the anthropologist argues, many items of behavior and belief are similarly governed by uniform rules. In fact, the rules of any language can be looked on as simply a particularly clear instance of the generalization that human social behavior in every society follows regular rules—customs, mores, standards, for different situations—that are learned by individuals as they grow up in their particular societies. The main details of the handling of boats, throwing of the nets, and hauling in of fish are likely to be very much the same for each group of fishermen in an Eskimo fishing village. It is not necessary for the anthropologist to take a poll of the fishermen to describe the chief elements of these activities.

This regular patterning of behavior in all human societies makes it possible for the individuals in each community to predict one another's behavior and interact for mutual satisfaction of interests. Even fights and warfare are carried out according to "rules" and customs. How angry the British redcoats were when they found that the American Revolutionists didn't behave according to accepted European customs of military behavior!

But recognition of the patterning of behavior has sometimes led anthropologists and others to give the impression that primitive and folk societies are slaves of custom and tradition, with little variation in behavior within local communities. Those individuals in primitive societies who seemed to vary from the dead level of average behavior have often been labeled "deviant" or "exceptional," thus preserving the illusion that most of the people in the tribe or village were pretty much alike.

THE ANTHROPOLOGIST AS "RESEARCH INSTRUMENT"

Social anthropologists have sometimes written their reports and books on primitive communities with a cavalier disregard for presentation of the evidence used to arrive at general conclusions. Some anthropologists have maintained that their generalizations about the personality, the emotional tone, the ethos of a particular way of life cannot be demonstrated objectively with systematic evidence. The reader must, in effect, trust to the honesty and objectivity of the anthropologist, much as the judgment of a work of art must be left to individual subjective experience.

This subjective element in anthropological field work has been under heavy attack. Critics have pointed out, for example, that earlier anthropologists, notably Ruth Benedict, described the Zuni and other Pueblo Indian ways of life as harmonious, moderate, peaceful—idyllic in every way imaginable. Later investigators, however, have accumulated evidence that these same Pueblo peoples are anxiety-ridden and quick to suspect and accuse one another of witchcraft. Given these discrepancies in reports by anthropologists on the Pueblo peoples, one might wonder whether there is anything about anthropological field work that is trustworthy.

Psychologists, sociologists, and others who expect almost all research information to be accompanied by statistical tables with appropriate calculations of averages and probabilities, point out that anthropological descriptions usually do not tell how many informants state a particular generalization; and all too often the anthropologist does not describe what individual behavior or statements led him to a particular generalization about the customs of a given people. Anthropologists have, at times, been somewhat careless, even secretive, about the nature of their field-work observations.

Facing up to these serious criticisms has resulted in a great deal of soul-searching and controversy within the ranks of anthropologists. Many of the criticisms concerning subjectivity and carelessness with evidence have been accepted as valid complaints, and anthropologists have searched for ways to overcome subjectivity in their methods. At the same time, they have tried to preserve those elements of anthropological method which were felt to be crucial to the scholarly tasks that anthropologists set for themselves.

In some areas of study, anthropologists have adopted the empirical techniques—particularly various tests—of other social scientists. In her study of the Alorese, mentioned earlier, Dr. Cora DuBois made extensive use of Rorschach projective tests, life histories, dreams of individuals, and analyses of drawings, in addition to gathering standard ethnographic data. She submitted the psychological materials to analysis by specialists, who interpreted the tests "blind"—that is, without knowledge of the cultural materials collected by the anthropologist.[1]

Other anthropological studies have introduced use of questionnaire schedules and careful sampling procedures borrowed from the methods of sociology (often in joint projects involving both sociologists and anthropologists). A comparative study of value orientations among the Zuni and Navaho Indians, Mormons, "Texans," and Spanish-Americans was undertaken in the southwestern United States by a team of anthropologists and sociologists.[2] A questionnaire was prepared, involving a series of situations, such as the following:

A man had a crop failure, or let us say, had lost most of his sheep or cattle. He and his family had to have help from someone if they were going to get through the winter. There are different ways of getting help. Which of these three ways would be best?

The three alternative answers posed for this question were supposed to indicate whether the respondent would 1) depend mostly on brothers and sisters and other relatives for help; 2) go to sources outside the local community for aid; or 3) turn for help to older important relatives or other local leaders who are used to managing things in his group.

Responses to the questions were collected from a sample of individuals in each of the five communities studied. These results were then carefully tabulated and analyzed statistically.

[1] *The People of Alor*, 2 vols. (paperback edition; New York: Harper and Row, 1960).
[2] Florence Kluckhohn and Fred Strodtbeck (eds.), *Variations in Value Orientations* (New York: Harper and Row, 1961).

In general, modern anthropological research shows increasing care in the presentation of evidence that can be independently examined and evaluated by other researchers.

SYNTHESIS OF ANTHROPOLOGICAL DATA

The heightened sophistication of anthropological field workers and the search for more objective research tools such as psychological tests, survey questionnaires, accurate censuses, and other techniques have greatly increased the usefulness of ethnographic reports brought back from the field. More and more, however, attention has shifted from problems of accurate reporting to the search for more accurate and useful historical and scientific generalizations from the information now available from hundreds of societies.

One important development of the past fifteen years is the growth of the cross-cultural (statistical) method for examining anthropological generalizations. Some anthropologists attempted cross-cultural studies decades ago, but this type of study has only recently begun to demonstrate its usefulness. Reasons for this success would appear to lie in the greatly increased numbers and quality of primary ethnographic reports, greater sophistication in formulation of questions for theoretical research, and improved methods of rapid collating of information, including use of electronic computers.

Until about fifteen years ago, any anthropologist who wanted to find out some piece of information from a sample of, say, sixty societies around the world, would have to read the individual field reports—the books, monographs, and research papers—on all the tribes in his sample. After laboriously searching through these individual works, he might still learn that much of the information he needed was missing. Since World War II, largely due to the efforts of Dr. George P. Murdock and his associates, the *Human Relations Area Files* (HRAF) have been established, in which information from hundreds of societies, from all the culture areas of the world, has been abstracted and assembled onto cards which are filed according to a master indexing system. For example, anyone wishing to find information on types of games played in societies around the world can go to the files, locate the appropriate index number, and gather together the required information in a fraction of the time it would have taken him to go to the original ethnographic sources. The HRAF files are now available at a number of the major universities in the United States.

A study by John W. M. Whiting and Irvin L. Child[3] offers a clear example of the cross-cultural method of anthropological study, making use of the HRAF files. The investigators were interested in examining the supposed influence of child training practices on adult customs in human societies. Using some ideas from Freudian psychoanalytic theory, modified by concepts from psychological learning theory, they hypothesized, for example, that in societies in which children are weaned early or harshly there is development of anxiety over oral activities that continues to be part of the personalities of the adults in the given society. Such anxiety about oral activities, they further reasoned, would lead to development of explanations of illnesses which emphasize oral activities—poison in one's food, eating the wrong kind of foods, and so on. To test this hypothesis (and a large number of similar hypotheses) Whiting and Child chose a sample of societies from the cross-cultural files and rated each society with respect to characteristics such as "severity of oral training" in childhood and also "oral explanations of illness."

The ratings of the researchers were then analyzed statistically. The results shown in Table 2 indicate support for the hypothesis that there is a relationship between the child training practice and customs concerning explanation of illness. A statistical calculation of probability for the results shown in Table 2 indicates that the striking relationships obtained (the clustering in cells B and C as compared with cells A and D) would happen by "sheer accident" less than 5 times in 10,000 attempts.

Many of the hypotheses tested by Whiting and Child did not yield results as striking as this one concerning oral anxiety, but in general their work lends support for the proposition that differences in child training practices are related to differences in adult customs. Other similarly organized studies have examined cross-cultural differences in drinking behavior, in use of "love magic," in beliefs in the helpfulness of deities, in types of kinship systems, and many other important questions.

Many anthropologists object to cross-cultural statistical studies, saying that such use of the ethnographic data removes the infor-

---

[3] *Child Training and Personality* (paperback edition; New Haven: Yale University, 1962).

TABLE 2

Relationship Between Oral Socialization Anxiety and Oral Explanations of Illness[4]

	Societies with oral explanations absent		*Societies with oral explanations present*	
	A		B	
Societies above average (median) on oral socialization anxiety	Lapps		Marquesans	Lesu
	Chamorro		Dobuans	Masai
	Samoans		Baiga	Lepcha
			Kwoma	Maori
			Thonga	Pukapukans
			Alorese	Trobrianders
			Chagga	Kwakiutl
			Navaho	Manus
			Dahomeans	
	C		D	
Societies below average (median) on oral socialization anxiety	Arapesh		Chiricahua	
	Balinese		Comanche	
	Hopi		Siriono	
	Tanala		Bena	
	Paiute		Slave	
	Chenchu		Kurtatchi	
	Teton			
	Papago			
	Flathead			
	Venda			
	Warrau			
	Wogeo			
	Ontong-Javanese			

mation too far from the behavioral context in which it occurs, making such information unreal, abstractified, or even downright false. Supporters of the method generally admit to weaknesses in the procedure, particularly in the availability and interpretation of the raw ethnographic reports, but feel that these cross-cultural studies test particular hypotheses that can be further studied by more intensive means in individual societies.

---

[4] *Ibid.*, p. 156.

SUMMARY AND CONCLUSIONS

In all phases of anthropological research there has been a great increase in the use of technical equipment: recording devices, complex photography, X-ray devices, sound spectrographs, and electronic computers. In the non-mechanized procedures of gathering data—in interviewing, "observing-while-participating," and digging—anthropologists have become much more sensitive to the necessity for rigorous, accurate description of the observations that lie back of ethnographic generalizations. There has been a great increase in use of statistics in the analysis of certain kinds of anthropological data. Generalizations that used to be regarded as unquestioned facts have been re-examined. Anthropology has become, in many respects, more scientifically "respectable." It is probable that anthropology will continue to combine some of the descriptive, holistic methods of the humanities with the more analytic and statistically-oriented practices of the social sciences.

Suggested Reading

*Malinowski, Bronislaw. *Argonauts of the Western Pacific*. New York: E. P. Dutton and Co., Inc., 1961.

This classic ethnographic report begins with a very important discussion of anthropological field-work methods.

Advanced Reading

*Moore, Frank W. *Readings in Cross-cultural Methodology*. New Haven: Human Relations Area Files Press, 1961.

These readings illustrate significant problems in the rapidly developing area of cross-cultural studies, usually involving the Human Relations Area Files as a basic source of ethnographic data.

*Tax, Sol (ed.). *Anthropology Today—Selections*. Chicago: University of Chicago Press, 1962.

Several papers on methods of research are included in this inventory volume.

---

* Paperback.

chapter four

Significant Research in Anthropology

Few people would deny that the "study of man" is concerned with phenomena of great complexity. In fact, many critics of the social sciences have claimed that human behavior is essentially beyond effective scientific study. According to this line of argument, the influence of man's "free will," and the enormous, apparently unlimited possibilities for variations in human behavior make the efforts of generalizing about man and culture essentially fruitless, if not dangerous. To make matters worse, there is the inevitable subjectivity of man studying himself—a problem not encountered by the physical scientists in their study of atoms, animals, and astrophysics.

Critics of the social sciences (including anthropology) can point to conflicting "facts," inconsistencies in terminology, and the seemingly hopeless divergences in theoretical assumptions as evidence of the obvious immaturity of these studies. Usually skeptics point for contrast to the great precision and elaborate mathematics found in physics and chemistry. They are quick to mention advances in communications systems, in automation of industry, and, more recently, in space technology as evidence of progress in the "real sciences"—progress that they believe the social sciences can never match. In comparison with the precision achieved in firing manned rockets into space, the scientific study of man seems most chaotic and unimpressive.

Anthropology, like the other social sciences, is a rather young discipline, and every field of scholarship must pass through a relatively long stage of growing up. The formative period of a science must involve collecting of much descriptive information; trial and error testing of methods and theories (with inevitable fads or temporary explorations); organization of preliminary classifica-

49

tions of "types " of subjects to be studied; and many other steps. In the later "mature phase," general principles and scientific laws can be developed. Much current anthropological study is still in the data-gathering and exploratory phases. However, the gathering of descriptive information about human history and peoples of the world is no small achievement in itself, and this store of information, once gathered, can be put to a variety of uses.

THE EVIDENCE OF HUMAN EVOLUTION

Some of man's tool-using, "ape-man" ancestors may have been living in East Africa almost two million years ago.[1] A new series of fossil discoveries from Tanganyika, announced by Dr. L. S. B. Leakey in the spring of 1964, has been assigned, tentatively, an age of 1,800,000 years. Dr. Leakey has found a number of fossils in the same area, and some of the remains of these man-ape creatures were found with crude stone tools—clear evidence of human-like culture. The ages of these important "new" fossils were established by the potassium-argon method (based on the breakdown, at a constant rate, of an unusual form of potassium, which gives off the gas, argon, and leaves ordinary potassium). Leakey named his latest discovery *Homo habilis* ("man with ability").

In South Africa, anthropologists and their colleagues have found dozens of fossil specimens of an ape-man that has been named *Australopithecus* ("southern ape"). In spite of the connotations of the name, there is much evidence that this little fellow walked upright (standing about four feet tall), used bones and stones for tools, had very humanlike face and teeth, and was equipped with a brain midway between that of the ape and modern man in size. These characteristics put *Australopithecus* on the borderline between man and ape. So far, then, it looks as if Africa may be the "birthplace of man."

The evidence amassed during the past century concerning the biological evolution of man is truly impressive. Fossilized skulls and other skeletal remains of early man have been found in hundreds of different locations throughout the world. The first evidence of Neandertal Man, found over a hundred years ago, has been supplemented by numbers of Neandertal finds in Germany, France, Spain, Italy, Yugoslavia, and Belgium. Neandertal-like fossils have also been found in Palestine, Africa, and in Southeast Asia, suggest-

---

[1] As reported in *Minneapolis Morning Tribune*, Saturday, April 4, 1964.

ing a fairly wide distribution around the world for this type of early man. Neandertal Man lived about 100,000 years ago—much more recently than *Australopithecus* and *Homo habilis*.

The links between Neandertal Man and the African fossil men are a series of fossils from East Asia, particularly the famed Java Man *(Pithecanthropus erectus)* and Peking Man. The remains of Peking Man were found with fairly strong evidence of human use of fire. Geological and other methods of dating all suggest that Java Man and similar early men were living on earth about 600,000 years ago. It is important to note that sizes of the brain cases of these fossils are about halfway between that of *Australopithecus* and modern man. A most important part of human biological evolution has been the steady increase in brain size and complexity.

Fossil evidence of fully modern man—*Homo sapiens*—is abundant in Europe, Asia, and Africa. These fossils are only 10,000 to 30,000 years old. Many anthropologists argue, therefore, that *Homo sapiens* evolved in fairly recent times. On the other hand, Dr. Leakey argues that his new East African discovery, *Homo habilis*, is quite "modern" in brain size and jaw structure, suggesting that *Homo sapiens* really was nearly fully developed over a million years ago.

The fossil men and remains of their cultures that have been found in the New World—North and South America—all tell the same story. The ancestors of American Indians came from Siberia perhaps less than 50,000 years ago. There were no man-apes in the Americas.

THE EVIDENCE OF HUMAN CULTURAL EVOLUTION

For more than a million years the ancestors of man lived as small bands of hunters and foragers, using only very simple stone, bone, and wooden weapons and implements. Very few important changes occurred in the cultural equipment of man's ancestors during those first million years, as far as can be determined from archaeological research. The rich stores of stone tools that constitute our main evidence for that early period in culture history show a very gradual refinement and specialization in man's equipment, from crude pebble-tools to carefully shaped handaxes.

Archaeological excavations in Western Europe provide evidence of significant development of cultural complexity near the end of the Ice Age. During the last 40,000 years of the Great Glaciation, the "cave men" who roamed what is now France and Spain developed a style in their cave paintings and other art work that still today ranks among man's greatest artistic achievements. On the walls of nearly inaccessible underground caverns they painted amazing polychrome representations of the mammoths, bison, reindeer, and other animals that they hunted. It is generally believed that these masterworks were produced for the practical purposes of hunting magic and ritual, rather than representing *l'art pour l'art*.

The truly revolutionary changes in human culture that make our complex modern life possible developed during the past 10,000 years—a tiny fraction of man's total cultural history. The series of inventions that radically changed man's way of living was the domestication of plants and animals. Excavations by Robert Braidwood and others in Iraq, Iran, and Israel have recently given us a much better picture of the probable beginnings of the "food-production revolution." Archaeological and botanical evidence strongly favors the Near East as the probable "birthplace" of agriculture, for many of the plants that man has learned to sow, care for, and harvest grow wild in that part of the world. In some sites in the same area, archaeologists have found stone "sickles" that were probably used for harvesting the wild plants in a time before men discovered ways to plant and cultivate crops for themselves.

Braidwood and his associates have carried out systematic investigation of the site of an ancient hillside village in Iraq.[2] This village, called Jarmo, appears to have been a cluster of about twenty-five mud houses. The people who lived there grew barley and wheat and kept some domestic animals, but also relied a great deal upon wild foods as well. These people, and people of similar ancient villages of the Near East, may have been the not-so-far-removed descendants of the world's first cultivators. From radiocarbon samples the remains of the village have been dated back about 8,500 years.

Little agricultural villages like Jarmo may have been only one or two steps removed from the hunting-and-foraging way of life, but those are mighty steps. Controlling their own food supply to a much greater degree than was possible for Stone Age hunters, these people could live in settled villages, could support a larger population, and had more leisure time. The leisure time could be used simply for loafing, but it also made possible the development of

[2] Robert J. Braidwood, "The Agricultural Revolution," *Scientific American*, CCIII, No. 3 (1960), 130–52.

new kinds of craftsmanship—pottery, weaving, tool-making, and other manufacturing. Given the fairly rich areas available for cultivation in the Near East, it was only a matter of time before the agriculturalists of the little hillside villages expanded their activities into the river valleys.

The world's first cities, several of them prominently mentioned in the Old Testament, were built in the fertile valleys of the Tigris and Euphrates rivers. Tremendous archaeological work has gone into the careful uncovering of evidence about the transition from little farming villages like Jarmo to the concentration of people in cities such as Al Ubaid, out of which grew Sumerian civilization. The cities were made possible by the invention of irrigation works in the river valleys, and it appears that those earliest cities were governed by theocracies of priests who controlled secular activities of food production and handicrafts, as well as the sacred ritual activities involving man's relationship with the supernatural beings.

Evidence unearthed so far indicates that those first cities developed about 4000 B.C. The evidence also shows that around that same time a great many striking new techniques and implements were invented by the people of the Mesopotamian region. Extraction and use of metals was invented, the making of bronze from a combination of tin and copper was developed, craftsmen began to do remarkably good work in manufacture of weapons, ornaments, tools, pottery, and other goods, and the record keepers for the priestly temples began to use more and more complicated marks for keeping track of grain receipts and other transactions. The first written language and mathematics came into being. The servants of the temples also developed accurate means of keeping track of the seasons by observing the movements of heavenly bodies. Astronomy, the oldest science, came into being, and with it, the first calendars.

The inventions and discoveries of the Mesopotamians spread widely in the Old World. From the archaeological evidence it appears likely that the ancient civilizations of Egypt, India, and even China were the result of the diffusion of those strategic inventions—agriculture, metal-working, and record-keeping—from the original cradle of civilization, Mesopotamia.

At the point at which the archaeological record of man's past gradually shades into the earliest dawn of written history, anthropologists and historians are greatly dependent on one another as they try to gain fuller knowledge of the rise of civilization.

TIME (APPROX.)	OLD WORLD	NEW WORLD
Now		
Birth of Christ		Aztec and Inca Empires Mayan Civilization
	Rise of Greek Civilization	
2,000 B. C.		Beginnings of Mayan Towns
	Invention of Metal Working, Writing, and Many Other New Things	
4,000 B. C.	First Cities in Mesopotamia	Invention of Maize-growing
	Invention of Grain-growing in Near East	
10,000 B. C.	Western European Cave Art	First Men Arrive in New World (by way of Alaska)
	Many New Forms of Stone Tools	
100,000 B. C.	Neandertal Man	
	Handaxes Found Widely in Old World	
500,000 B. C.	Java Man and Peking Man Fossils (and many stone tools)	
1 Million B. C.	Crude Stone Tools of Man Found in Africa and in Europe	
1.7 Million B. C.	Australopithecus and Homo Habilis Found with Stone Tools at Oldavai Gorge in East Africa by Leakey	

Figure 2. **The History of Human Cultural and Biological Evolution—as Read from the Anthropological Evidence (read from the bottom up).**

54

Aztec and Inca Empires
Mayan Civilization

Birth of Christ

Rise of Greek
Civilization

First Cities in Mesopotamia

4,000 B. C.

2,000 B. C.

Western European
Cave Art

Invention of Maize-
growing in New World

Invention of
Grain-growing in Near East

20,000 B. C.

Neandertal Man

Many New Forms
of Stone Tools

First Arrivals in
New World (via Alaska)

Handaxes
in Old World

100,000 B. C.

500,000 B. C.
Java Man and
Peking Man Fossils
Many Stone Tools

1 Million B. C.
Crude Stone Tools
Africa and Europe

1.7 Million B. C.
Australopithecus and
Homo Habilis
Oldavai Gorge

Man's Trek—as Read from the Anthropological Evidence.

55

The influence of Mesopotamian civilization apparently had very little to do with the rise of Mayan, Aztec, and Inca civilizations of the New World. The archaeological materials tell the story of an independent development, involving a set of inventions and discoveries different from those of the Near East. Quite different foods were cultivated—maize, beans, squash, tomatoes, and potatoes, all of which were unknown in the Old World until the time of Columbus; and metal-working, writing, mathematics, calendars, astronomy, and other achievements appear to have been developed out of local traditions, rather than being carried from the distant civilizations of Mesopotamia and Egypt. The remarkable achievements of the American Indians took place several thousand years later than similar growth in the Near East. In fact, much of the growth of Middle American and Peruvian (Inca) civilizations took place within the past 2,000 years. A summary of the main developments in the history of man is presented in Figure 2.

OTHER EVIDENCE CONCERNING HUMAN CULTURE HISTORY

As we approach more recent times, the archaeological and fossil evidence are supported more and more by other kinds of information.

Careful measurement and observations of living human populations lend support to the view that most of the peoples of Europe, the Near East, and India are related to one another as descendants of one branch—the Caucasoid stock—of *Homo sapiens*. The prehistoric background of other areas also can be illuminated by examination of the data from physical anthropology. For example, the American Indians are most closely related biologically to the Mongoloid peoples of Northeast Asia, adding to the weight of evidence underlying the proposition that the Americas were settled from Asia by way of the Bering Straits.

Linguistic studies have shown that most of the peoples of Europe and India speak related languages—all of the Indo-European language family. Meticulous comparative studies of these languages make possible the reconstruction of portions of the language of the Indo-European ancestor. These vocabulary reconstructions provide evidence for inferences about the economic system, family structure, food habits, and other aspects of the culture of the ancient Indo-Europeans. Naturally, the linguistic and biological data are most usually examined in conjunction with archaeological information. Careful sifting of linguistic, archaeological, and biological evidence about culture history is especially important for those parts of the world in which there has been little written history until recent times. Maps of related language groupings, the occurrence of particular complexes of cultural traits, together with archaeological evidence, have helped to reconstruct some outlines of the prehistory of Africa, the Americas, and other parts of the world. Evidence from language and culture are the main sources of information about the almost unbelievable migrations of Polynesians and related peoples throughout the islands of the South Seas. People with Malayo-Polynesian languages and related customs are found all the way from Madagascar, off the east coast of Africa, to Easter Island (which belongs to Chile) —a distance of over 13,000 miles, or more than halfway around the globe! To travel such wide spans of ocean these peoples had only their little sailing canoes.

THE DATA ON HUMAN BEHAVIOR

The masses of information that anthropologists have collected about the peoples of the world always point in two directions. Looking backward, we are naturally interested in tracing man's biological and cultural history, as outlined above. The same information, however, is also the raw material from which we seek to put together generalizations about human behavior. We want to understand modern human behavior in all its forms, rather than merely to learn some interesting facts about the past.

Now, if a biologist were searching for generalizations about the behavior of birds, it is unlikely that he would rely upon data limited to descriptions of the behavior of birds of North America. Similarly, no sensible oceanographer attempts to study the characteristics of the oceans using only information from the North Atlantic. These scientists search out the fullest possible information from all parts of our globe when pursuing study of their favorite subject. It therefore seems strange to anthropologists that there have been so many studies made and books written about human nature, religion, law, art, and other aspects of man using information from one small subgroup of humans—namely, Americans and Europeans.

The tendency of many scholars to generalize about man's ways from such a narrow sampling of the available evidence appears to be due to two main factors. First, information about the beliefs, institutions, marriage patterns, economic systems, and personalities of the great variety of non-European peoples has not been easily available to everyone. Until about 100 years ago there was no systematically collected mass of ethnographic data. The second, and perhaps more important reason, is that all men everywhere tend to view their own way of life as the most reasonable and natural—as exemplary of human behavior at its best. It is not surprising, therefore, that even the most profound philosophers of both East and West have commonly derived their theories of human nature from study of their own countrymen and neighboring nations, deeming the customs of more distant peoples as savage, quaint, barbaric, illogical, unnatural, or even subhuman.

As early as the seventeenth and eighteenth centuries, however, some European philosophers began to use information about the Red Indians and the people of the South Seas as evidence for their theories. J. J. Rousseau's use of ethnographic materials for his concept of the "noble savage" is an example of this tendency. The ethnographic information available to these men was, of course, rather scanty and inaccurate, since it had been collected in an unorganized manner by a variety of travelers, adventurers, missionaries, and others, as a sideline to their major activities and interest. The philosophers could hardly draw useful conclusions about human nature when their ethnographic sources told of one-eyed giants, tribes with mouths in the middle of their stomachs, people without either language or religion, and other fantasies.

Only in the twentieth century has the level of ethnographic information so improved that the more striking absurdities have been dropped from common belief, and something approaching accurate descriptions of human lifeways have become available from the important geographical sub-areas of the world. Even today there are great gaps in the availability of particular kinds of information. To give just one example, only since about 1945 have anthropologists made serious attempts to gather systematic data on child-rearing practices.

Widespread recognition among non-anthropologists of the importance of cross-cultural materials for generalizations about human behavior has developed only in the past twenty-five years. Almost anyone writing today on such subjects as religious systems, the human family, personality development, or law-ways, feels compelled to take notice of at least some of the rich store of relevant information from non-Western societies.

PROMISING DEVELOPMENTS IN ANTHROPOLOGICAL THEORY

The accumulation of descriptive information about human behavior, past and present, has now reached proportions which make possible significant advances in anthropological theory. One of the perennially favorite topics of anthropological theory has been the question of cultural evolution—the search for general stages or regular patterns in human culture history. After the nineteenth-century version of cultural evolution had been thoroughly discredited, most anthropologists avoided—almost as a kind of supernatural taboo—any examination of cultural evolutions. In more recent times, there have been serious attempts to build new theories on better foundations.

Julian Steward has advanced a theory that he calls "multilinear evolution." [3] Instead of assuming that human lifeways everywhere advance through similar sequences of progress from "savagery" to "civilization," Steward has searched for more limited parallels among societies developing in comparable environmental situations. Looking at the rise of civilizations in Mesopotamia, Egypt, China, Peru, and Middle America, Steward (along with other anthropologists) has noted that quite similar processes of cultural growth took place in these widely separated circumstances. The "formative period" in each of these areas was marked by development of metallurgy, population growth, expansion of the dominant culture, building of large irrigation works, and appearance of multi-community "state" organization. Steward's theories suggest that the development of complex societies in other kinds of natural environments (e.g., Northern Europe) would be expected to take different patterns from the ones just described. This theoretical framework assumes that cultural processes must be studied as an interaction among environment, social organization, technological inventory, and ideological patterns—acting upon and influencing each other as men adapt to given environments and try to improve their conditions of living.

---

[3] *Theory of Culture Change* (Urbana: University of Illinois Press, 1955).

Many of the earlier anthropological descriptions of particular peoples were presented merely as lists of the various "peculiar" customs found in the particular society, with little conception of how these customs were related to one another, or how the society practicing them was organized.

Emerging anthropological theory is based on the general postulate that different customs and behaviors within a given society are functionally interrelated. Further, anthropologists assume that any community of people can be described as organized into a social system in which individuals and groups play various parts, or "roles," in the drama of living. These basic assumptions can be employed in the study of any aspect of human cultural or social organization.

Anthropological research shows that the conjugal family— man and wife, plus children—is a fundamental unit in nearly all human societies. In addition to this core unit, however, societies differ widely in the ways and the extent to which kinship relationships are organizing principles for larger social units. Some very large tribes (especially in Africa) are politically and socially organized mainly into bodies of patrilineal kinsmen (group membership reckoned through males only); other tribes of the same size have kings and political administrations based on non-kinship relationships. Many societies that practice hoe-cultivation of crops, as in South America, Africa, and elsewhere, have matrilineal kin groups (group membership reckoned through females). Again, many of the world's peoples consider paternal and maternal kinsmen of equal importance in the formation of social groups and alliances.

As a general rule, it can be said that development of complex, industrial societies has brought an increase in the varieties of non-kinship social groupings (clubs, associations, unions, corporations, etc.). But many primitive societies also have "clubs," craft guilds, religious societies, and other groupings of non-kin; and family and kinship relations still provide the foundations for important elements of human behavior in complex modern societies.

Much anthropological research has recently gone into the examination of beliefs in magic and witchcraft. Educated representatives of our own way of life generally regard these elements of "superstition" as clear evidence of backwardness and irrationality. Missionaries, governmental agents, and others campaign against the magical beliefs and witchcraft practices of Australian aborigines, Africans, and American Indians, often without much apparent success. Usually, those who have sought to stamp out

such practices have naively regarded these ideas as simply rem-
nants of pagan beliefs—relics of the past.

As we noted in Chapter 2, it was Bronislaw Malinowski who
first clearly suggested and produced evidence for the relationship
between magical practices and life's areas of uncertainty.[4] Those
pulse-quickening situations in hunting, warfare, ocean sailing, or
other activities where a man's technical abilities are insufficient
to affect the uncontrollables of weather, wild animals, stormy seas,
dangerous enemies—these are the kinds of situations in which
men everywhere turn to wish-projections in the form of magical
practices. Malinowski saw this response to anxiety as a natural
attribute of all humans, including both the Trobriand sailor on
the high seas and the modern American embarking on unusually
difficult action. Everyone does not incline to magical practices to
the same degree, but examples from our own modern society
support Malinowski's theory. In- areas where our abilities and
technology are in doubt—in struggles with incurable illnesses, the
dangers of warfare, and even in the uncertainties of hardfought
ballgames—we "moderns" easily show interest in rabbits' feet,
lucky talismans of all sorts, mystical quack medicines, magical
avoidance of certain words and dozens of other little rituals. Even
religious conversions and visionary experiences appear related to
intense anxieties. It would be very interesting to compile materials
on the magical practices employed by college students at examination time—the most anxiety-ridden situation in the academic world!

In an excellent study of two West African societies, S. F.
Nadel has demonstrated that accusations of witchcraft tend to be
leveled at the people in society who are the most anxiety-provoking
in their behavior.[5] Among the Nupe people of Nigeria, for example,
there is much tension between men and their wives. The women,
who often have more wealth than the men, frequently engage in
trading and shopping expeditions away from their families and
express their independence in a number of other ways that run
counter to the accepted Nupe standards for virtuous and dutiful
women. The analysis shows that ambivalence toward women is at
least part of the explanation for the fact that females are much
more often accused of witchcraft than are males. Furthermore, the
accusations of witchcraft may serve to keep the females somewhat

---

[4] In *Magic, Science, and Religion* (New York: The Free Press of Glencoe,
1948).

[5] "Witchcraft in Four African Societies," *American Anthropologist*, LIV
(1952), 18–29.

under the control of the insecure males, for witchcraft is a serious crime, and steps are taken to punish the alleged offenders.

Guy Swanson has examined a sample of fifty societies in terms of the hypothesis that witchcraft tends to be prevalent when people must interact with one another on important matters in the absence of legitimated social controls and arrangements. He divided his fifty societies into those having important legitimated social controls in most relationships and those in which such controls were lacking, and found a much higher prevalence. of witchcraft beliefs in the latter group.

TABLE 3

Relationship of Witchcraft Beliefs to Presence of Legitimated Social Controls[6]

Prevalence of Witchcraft	Societies Having Legitimated Social Controls	Societies Having Unlegitimated or Uncontrolled Relationships
High	1	17
Intermediate	14	7
Low	9	1

In the language of statisticians, these figures could have occurred simply by chance only 5 times in 10,000. Thus we have strong reasons to believe that there is a relationship between witchcraft and type of social control.

The importance of these findings about magic and witchcraft is greatly increased when we realize that similar phenomena occur in our modern society. Here, however, the "magical" ideas are often translated into twisted beliefs about Communism, fear of fluoridation, scapegoating of minority groups, weird distortions about "what goes on in our universities," and many other puzzling conceptions. From the cross-cultural anthropological evidence as well as from psychological studies, it appears that people who experience fear and frustrations in their daily lives often develop "magical" beliefs about the sources of their problems. They then project the blame onto "witches," who in our modern society may

[6] Reprinted from *The Birth of the Gods,* pp. 137 ff., by Guy E. Swanson, by permission of the University of Michigan Press. Copyright © 1960. All rights reserved.

be racial or religious minorities, the government, the politicians, "Communists and other radicals," "those atheists in the university," or other identifiable groups.

As has already been suggested, many of these studies showing strong evidence of the interrelatedness of various human behaviors and beliefs have been produced as a result of the application of psychological principles to analysis of customary behavior.

The study of child training practices by Whiting and Child, which we examined in Chapter 3, is another example of this tendency in anthropological studies. The interaction between anthropological and psychological ideas is a two-way street, however, as is richly illustrated in recent progress in mental health studies.

For example, anthropologists have produced much evidence showing that: (a) mental illness takes different forms in different societies; (b) different societies have different ways of defining what is abnormal behavior; and (c) different peoples have different rates of mental disorder. Some societies in Africa, for example, have very low rates of suicide but have frequent manic outbursts among individuals. On the other hand, certain European societies show a very high suicide and depression rate, with less show of manic outbursts.

Many peoples consider it normal for individuals to experience hallucinations, visions, and trances. Among the people of Bali, for example, several major ceremonies include trance behavior as a regular part of the ritual. The shaman, or medicine man, in many American Indian groups and in Siberia and other parts of the world, regularly gives performances including trance states, hallucinations, and unconsciousness. This behavior among ordinary members of our own society might often lead to a diagnosis of mental instability. However, some small religious sects in American society do regularly become "possessed" and experience trances as part of their religious services. The fact that behavior considered "abnormal" in one society is considered quite "normal" in another raises serious problems for any pan-human concepts of mental health and mental disorder. In this kind of problem, psychiatric and psychological theory has been modified by the cross-cultural findings of the anthropologists. In spite of difficulties in defining what is abnormal or unhealthy personality, most observers are now in agreement that *all* societies have *some* individuals who can be diagnosed clearly as mentally ill, and are so classified by the local people themselves.

Alexander and Dorothea Leighton and their associates have been carrying on an extensive research project in Nova Scotia concerning the relationship between rates of mental illness and types of communities. Their research indicates so far that communities showing relatively greater "social disorganization" have greater numbers of mentally disturbed individuals in the local population.[7] Here, again, anthropological research has amassed evidence for the interrelatedness of community organization, personality characteristics, local customary behavior, religious beliefs, and other elements of peoples' lifeways. Many of the large-scale mental health research projects of recent years have involved close co-operation of anthropologists, psychologists, psychiatrists, and sociologists.

SUMMARY

Anthropology is rather young among established academic studies and cannot claim to have produced extensive and elaborate laws or generalizations about human behavior analogous to the laws and principles of, for example, chemistry, astronomy, or physics. Much of the hundred years or so of anthropological study has been devoted to the very important task of accumulating information—the raw material about human customs and characteristics from which a mature theoretical system can be constructed.

The achievements of anthropology in the collection of discriptive materials have been considerable. Most apparent to the modern educated world is the great mass of information we now have for reconstruction of "what happened in history"—the main outlines of human biological and cultural evolution from simple beginnings over a million years ago. Both human fossil materials and archaeological data supply us with the information for this aspect of anthropological interest.

Ethnographic collections about the great variety of human behavior and customs throughout the world represent another notable achievement of this first descriptive phase of the study of anthropology. Any generalizations about economic systems, religious beliefs, "human nature," etc., can now be built on the foundations of wide-ranging ethnographic information on hundreds of different societies.

---

[7] In *The Character of Danger* (New York: Basic Books, Inc., 1963).

Theoretical developments in anthropology are now beginning to emerge, developed from the accumulated descriptive ethnographies. Refinements in research on cultural evolution have been developed, and a major theoretical structure for understanding the functional organization of human behavior systems is emerging from study of the interrelations of belief systems with elements of social organization and economic arrangements. Many of the important contributions to this growing theoretical system depend on application of psychological concepts and other theoretical ideas borrowed from related social sciences.

Suggested Reading

*Leakey, L. S. B. *Adam's Ancestors*. New York: Harper Torchbooks, 1963.

The discoverer of the very important fossil remains in East Africa writes from a lifetime of research in Old World physical anthropology and archaeology.

*Linton, Ralph. *The Tree of Culture* (abridged). New York: Vintage Books, 1959.

Ralph Linton surveys the culture history and ethnographic data of the major cultural areas of the world in a very readable and interesting way.

*MacGowan, Kenneth, and Joseph A. Hester, Jr. *Early Man in the New World*. ("The Natural History Library"), Garden City: Doubleday and Co., Inc., 1962.

This good-humored account of New World fossil and archaeological remains also includes an excellent introduction to Old World prehistory as background to the arrival of early man in the Americas.

*Spindler, George and Louise (eds.). *Case Studies in Cultural Anthropology*. New York: Holt, Rinehart & Winston, Inc. (series began in 1960).

This series of paperbacks now consists of a number of compact (about 100 pages each), highly readable ethnographic

---

* Paperback.

accounts of societies such as the Cheyenne, the Tiwi of Australia, two African native kingdoms (Swazi and Bunyoro), a Greek village, a village in India, and Tepoztlan (a Mexican village). Each culture is described by an anthropologist who carried out field work in that society.

Advanced Reading

*Dobzhansky, Theodosius. *Mankind Evolving*. New Haven and London: Yale University Press, 1962.

The data on biological evolution, human genetics, and effects of culture on natural selection are woven together into an important new view of man's biological present and future.

*DuBois, Cora. *The People of Alor*. New York: Harper Torchbooks, 1960.

This two-volume work is one of the best available examples of a "culture-and-personality" study of a society.

*Firth, Raymond. *We the Tikopia*. Boston: Beacon Press, 1963 (first published in 1936).

The Tikopia live on a small, isolated island in the South Pacific. Raymond Firth, a student of Malinowski and now one of the most distinguished of British social anthropologists, has described these island people with the same thoroughness and methodological rigor that his mentor spent on the Trobriand Islanders.

For the reader who wishes to build a library of anthropological materials, it may be mentioned that a large and rapidly growing selection of anthropological works is available in paperback editions.

chapter five

Fundamental
Insights from
Anthropological
Research

Many hundreds of thousands of years ago, a "man-ape" sort of creature developed innovations in physical characteristics that made possible a complex speech system, symbolic manipulation of ideas, and much increased storage of information in the brain. Thus man came into being. Through a very gradual evolutionary process, man became increasingly differentiated from the apes and began to shape his lifeways by social traditions, learned behavior, and complex symbolic interaction.

THE CONCEPT OF CULTURE

"Culture" is the word we use to label the "something that was added" that accounts for the large differences in behavior distinguishing man from all the other animals. Culture often means simply the "social heritage" of a given group of people. The social heritage is not a "thing" that is handed down intact, like a hope chest, from generation to generation. It is rather the complex abstraction we could build if it were possible to put together the ideas, patterns of meaning, and "rules" for behavior of all the individuals in a given community. Each new generation reshuffles and changes the systems of ideas, meanings, and rules, so that the social tradition is never fixed and unchanging in any society. Most anthropologists would agree that recognition of the nature and importance of culture is the single most important insight that has marked the development of the study of man.

In studying and comparing cultures both primitive and civilized, we have found that practically all the important differ-

67

ences in lifeways of Americans, Chinese, Australian aborigines, Eskimos, Pygmies of the Congo, and other peoples are understandable as *differences in learned patterns of social behavior,* not differences in biological apparatus, type of brain, type of blood, or any other genetically inherited mechanisms. There is, then, no need to wonder at the idea of "cannibals' sons going to Oxford," as one writer recently put it.

The concept of culture has, of course, become commonly accepted among educated people today, so that it is difficult to realize that only fifty or sixty years ago many scholars still believed the notion that the differences in behavior of Europeans represented different biologically inherited characteristics of the "German race," the "French race," the "English race," and so forth. Recent studies and recent history have demonstrated that individuals from simple cultures, even of "Stone Age culture," become Westernized and adapted to modern culture in incredibly short spans of time; and we are aware that our own Western culture is undergoing rapid change. All of these developments highlight the extremely adaptable nature of human cultural behavior.

POSTULATES OF ANTHROPOLOGY

Our understanding of the general history of science has reached a point where we are well aware that today's accepted fundamental principles are often found tomorrow to be quaint misconceptions of immature scholarship. Therefore, the postulates given below should be looked at critically, with a readiness to discard any or all of them when they have outlived their usefulness. At present, these statements appear to be supported by much available evidence, and they seem to be helpful guides for research and study in anthropology and related subjects.

1. Culture is a total lifeway, not just a superficial set of customs. It largely shapes how man feels, behaves, and perceives as he adapts to his world.

Some earlier scholars took the view that the "customs" of various people are simply a random collection of peculiar beliefs and quaint practices that are a sort of overlay, a more or less colorful glaze, on the outer surface of "natural man." Now we realize that among primitive and civilized peoples alike, our social heritage strongly influences how we perceive and categorize all experience. Even our biological functioning is much shaped by culture. We get hungry at certain times of the day (in different cultures it occurs at different times) because our cultural learning has trained our physiological processes to react at regular "meal times." Our perceptions of sounds, colors, and other "natural" phenomena are conditioned by social experience. Many of the peoples of the world (e.g., the Navaho of the Southwest) do not distinguish between green and blue in their language, apparently because their environments make such distinctions relatively insignificant. On the other hand, Americans lump under the single word *snow* everything from slush to "dry-powdery" in a range of travel conditions that must be carefully distinguished by separate words among the Eskimo, whose lives are greatly influenced by differences in kinds of snow.

Perhaps even more striking is our growing realization that illness is culturally defined and in many ways strongly influenced by cultural patterns. Psychosomatic ailments of all kinds illustrate for us the close interrelations among thoughts, beliefs, and bodily processes. Research in mental health has demonstrated great cultural differences within American society in the interpretation of psychological conditions. In different segments of the American population the same or nearly the same pattern of behavioral characteristics is interpreted in such phrases as "he's psychoneurotic," "he's just acting contrary," "the devil is tempting him," "he is evil," and many other variations.

Culture can kill!—and how different are the situations in various societies that can bring a person to commit suicide. In some societies the jilted lover is the most likely candidate to take his own life; in others it is the recipient of strong criticism from his father. In some societies suicide is so rare that the possible motivations for such an act are little understood by the people.

Well-authenticated cases of "voodoo death" (death by black magic) from various parts of the world provide us with another striking example of the power of cultural belief. It appears that the victim of black magic experiences profound psychophysiological shock when he learns that he has been "attacked" by a sorcerer. He loses appetite for food and water; blood pressure is reduced, blood plasma escapes into the tissues, and the heart deteriorates. He dies of shock that is physiologically the same as "wound shock" in war and highway casualties.

2. *Every cultural system is an interconnected series of ideas and patterns for behavior in which changes in one aspect generally lead to changes in other segments of the system.*

We now have much evidence that in every society the techniques and actions involved in food-getting are closely related to the social organization of the society. For example, most societies in which there is heavy reliance on animal husbandry tend to emphasize the dominance of males, as expressed in inheritance of property through males, and patrilocal choice of residence on marriage. Again, the ethnographic evidence suggests that foraging (hunting and gathering) societies tend to have more lenient child-rearing practices than do agricultural and pastoral peoples. We have noted in the previous chapter how the areas of religious and magical belief appear to be linked to other aspects of social organization.

Studies of changes introduced into primitive societies have demonstrated that it is practically impossible to introduce even the simplest technological innovations without affecting other areas of culture as well. A study of the introduction by missionaries and traders of steel axes into a stone axe-using Australian society showed that far-reaching social changes resulted from this supposedly simple technological change.[1] The stone axes of the traditional culture had been very important, scarce status symbols, owned and controlled by the old men of high prestige and power. The new steel axes upset the entire power system by putting efficient, high-status goods in the hands of women and young men, who had previously occupied subservient positions in the society.

Even games and pastimes, which are often assumed to be trivial, secondary items of behavior, are apparently linked to particular types of social systems. Recent research indicates that practically none of the simpler societies have developed games of strategy. Apparently, societies must have a certain minimum of hierarchical social complexity before problems of strategy become fascinating and entertaining to individuals. Simple hunting and gathering peoples seem to be more attracted to games that capitalize on physical prowess.[2]

---

[1] Lauriston Sharp, "Steel Axes for Stone Age Australians," in *Human Problems in Technological Change,* ed. Edward H. Spicer (New York: Russell Sage Foundation, 1952).
[2] John M. Roberts, Malcolm J. Arth, and Robert R. Bush, "Games in Culture," *American Anthropologist,* LXI (1959), 597–605.

3. Every human cultural system is logical and coherent in its own terms, given the basic assumptions and knowledge available to the given community.

This is mainly a restatement and summary of some points that have already been made, but it deserves repeating in order to lay to rest some earlier ideas that assigned to non-European peoples a "prelogical" or childlike failure to draw appropriate conclusions from experience.

Anthropological field workers have been unable to find any peoples in our world whose systems of reasoning or learning from experience could be called "illogical." The differences in thinking between "primitive man" and "modern man" appear to lie in their fundamental assumptions about the world and things in it, conditioned by differences in available information. Modern man "knows" that the earth revolves around the sun, rather than *vice versa*, because of the complex instruments of observation and calculation that have enabled a very few men in Western civilization to derive a fairly believable theory concerning the solar system. Most primitive peoples are in the position of relying on their eyes alone, according to which it is perfectly reasonable to regard the sun as the moving element, circling the stationary, possibly flat, earth.

Explanations of disease are another familiar area in which modern man has come to have some advantages over non-European thinkers. No primitive man has ever seen a germ. With no "objective" evidence pointing to the physical entities (germs) that have direct causal relationship to illness, primitive man has generally relied on his basic assumption about the universe: the world is full of supernatural spirits and powers which often cause trouble, including illness. If one granted this first premise, it then follows that illness should be treated by means of praying to, cajoling, placating, or driving out the guilty supernaturals. Primitive medical practices therefore make logical sense, granted the fundamental premises. Since most people recover from illness regardless of how they are treated, primitive men have generally had "objective evidence" testifying to the effectiveness of their curing methods.

Concerning mental illness, primitive medicine is even more interesting, for in that area the non-Western medicine man has apparently enjoyed considerable success, and non-Western concepts of therapy have in many areas anticipated modern psychiatric theory. The Iroquois Indians, for example, had in earlier times a winter ceremony in which persons with obsessive dreams and other psychological problems were permitted to act out their compulsions, after their dreams had been interpreted for them by tribal "psychoanalysts."[3] It is instructive to note that primitive medicine men appear to have had, and in some areas still have, therapeutic effectiveness with mental illness that compares favorably with that of modern psychiatry. Such therapeutic effectiveness is not, of course, proof of the correctness of the theories of either group.

Concerning the logic of the "civilized man" versus that of the "primitive," Leopold Pospisil quotes a Papuan native in a "Stone Age" society that was still mainly unaffected by Western culture at the time of his field work in 1955.

> How can you think [asked the native] that a man can sin and can have a free will, and at the same time believe that your God is omnipotent, and that he created the world and determined all the happenings? If he determined all that happens, and [therefore] also the bad deeds, how can a man be held responsible? Why, if he is omnipotent, did the Creator have to change himself into a man and allow himself to be killed [crucified] when it would have been enough for him just to order men to behave?" [4]

The man added that the Christian notion of man resembling God in appearance seemed to him utterly "stupid."

Members of Western society have tended to consider "rationality" in terms of economic self-interest. One branch of Western thinking, economics, has built up an hypothesis of "economic man" as the basis for analysis of important social processes, and many theoreticians have come to think of "economic man" as the model for judgment of human rationality.

It seems that the assumption of "economic man" works relatively well for predicting very gross trends in our own large-scale economy, but it does not appear to be wholly realistic as a yardstick in analysis of many situations in American society. For example, according to assumptions about economically rational man, working people leave areas of unemployment to move to areas of better employment possibilities. Why, then, do not all the economically deprived people of the Appalachian region leave for areas of

[3] Anthony F. C. Wallace, "The Institutionalization of Cathartic and Control Strategies in Iroquois Religious Psychotherapy," in *Culture and Mental Disorder*, ed. M. K. Opler (New York: The Macmillan Co., 1959), pp. 63–96.
[4] In *The Kapauku Papuans of West New Guinea* (New York: Holt, Rinehart & Winston, Inc., 1963), p. 85.

better employment possibilities? Again, during periods when there is a relatively saturated labor market in some urban centers of the United States, why do people from some rural areas continue to migrate to these urban centers, where they will have great difficulty in finding employment?

Modern man decides his actions from a very complex array of economic and noneconomic motives, including his emotional attachment to his home and his fear of unknown areas. The economic behavior of non-Western man, too, is based on intelligent seeking of economic advantage, plus a wide array of other, more obscure but understandable motives concerning emotional attachment to home area, loyalty to kinsmen, fear of demands of kinsmen, anxieties about the attitudes of supernatural entities (both his own and white man's gods), and many other motives.

4. The customs and beliefs of peoples are often made more understandable by studying them in terms of the social interrelations among types of individual and group statuses and roles in social action.

Painful ritual circumcision, knocking out of front teeth, other physical "hazing"; the complex of myth-enforced chanting and dancing; assigning of new names to neophytes; and other features of male initiation rites in many societies may seem at first impression senseless and barbaric practices. If they are regarded simply as customs unrelated to other elements of cultural organization, we can derive little understanding of these ceremonies. But these and other sorts of rituals begin to make sense as human acts when we view them as symbolic dramatizations of important status transitions experienced by individuals in the cycle of birth-maturity-death. It remains, then, to examine the particular characteristics of societies with initiation rites to find what special social and psychological characteristics seem especially to account for these ceremonies. One explanation, supported by statistical evidence, finds painful initiation of youths to be related to household arrangements that develop strong cross-sex identification of boys with their mothers.[5] Such household structures are found, for example, in polygynous societies and in societies where married men sleep in "men's houses" while the women and children sleep in their own separate quarters. For boys to become men in such societies, a traumatic "rebirth"

---

[5] John M. Whiting *et al.*, "The Function of Male Initiation Ceremonies at Puberty," in *Readings in Social Psychology*, eds. Maccoby, Newcomb, and Hartley (New York: Holt, Rinehart & Winston, Inc., 1958), pp. 359–70.

accompanied by much symbolizing of new status, is enacted. This kind of analysis of male initiation rites also points to another important general insight that has emerged in the study of anthropology:

5. *The customs and beliefs of peoples are often made more understandable if we examine them from a combined psychological and cultural perspective.*

In addition to the psychological inferences used above in analysis of rituals of status transition, we have noted (in Chapter 4) how beliefs in witchcraft and sorcery are understandable in relation to the anxieties and personality tensions of individuals. Behavior ranging from "mother-in-law avoidance" to complex ceremonies of "ritual rebellion" can be put in clearer perspective by careful interrelating of psychological theory with cultural and social observations. Often this kind of analysis requires use of psychological testing techniques.

6. *Analysis of the implications (or "functions") of cultural behavior must take into account the explicit beliefs and intentions of the people involved; but analysis must also be made of the unnoticed, unintended, further consequences (called "latent functions") of particular acts and beliefs.*

One illuminating example of this principle can be drawn from a look at the custom of binding infants in cradleboards among peoples of the British Columbia coastal area.[6] Among some of these Indians, the custom of binding infants tightly in cradleboards was explained as a beauty measure. It flattened the back of the skulls of infants in a way that was considered handsome by the people. When the custom fell into disuse an important unnoticed latent function of cradleboards was discovered. The cradleboard is a simple baby-tending device! When infants of crawling age were no longer kept in cradleboards, their mothers found themselves with the new task of watching to see that the baby did not crawl into the fire or fall into the nearby water. The Indian mothers did not, therefore, go back to using cradleboards (partly because they are considered "primitive" by Whites), but new patterns of child-tending had to be developed.

---

[6] From Clellan S. Ford as cited by Ward Goodenough in *Cooperation in Change* (New York: Russell Sage Foundation, 1963).

7. *Study of practically any behaviors and beliefs among primitive peoples, no matter how unusual, is of direct relevance to understanding our own complex culture, for it appears that humans everywhere shape their beliefs and behavior in response to the same fundamental human problems.*

All humans everywhere seek to eat and drink enough, to get shelter from danger and physical discomfort, to secure favorable reactions from their fellows, to be comforted when sick, threatened, or anxious, and to find satisfying explanations for phenomena in the observed world. The solutions to these human problems are of enormous variety, but they all give us clues to the nature of man as a cultural animal.

Human cultural behavior is extremely flexible, so that people have often developed quite different solutions to essentially similar problems. This is a reason why cultures have not all developed through identical, fixed stages of evolution, as the nineteenth-century evolutionists believed. But there is much evidence for the psychic and cultural oneness of mankind:

   a. Striking parallels are found in cultural sequences independently developed in the early civilizations of the Old and the New World. (See pp. 53–56.)
   b. There are a large number of cultural "universals" such as language, kinship systems, modesty concerning natural functions, regulation of sexual behavior, use of fire, naming of individuals, belief in a supernatural world, music and other arts, and dozens of other cultural patterns.
   c. The cross-cultural statistical studies (e.g., as described on pp. 45–47) show correlations among human cultural traits that appear to be based on some sort of psychic unity.
   d. Anthropologists have found no people whose system of language and logic was incomprehensible.

8. *Explanation of human behavior is essentially one-sided and incomplete unless information about man's biological, cultural, social, and psychological characteristics is taken into account, together with information about man's biophysical environment.*

This fundamental insight provides the rationale for the holistic, integrating style of scholarship that characterizes the study of anthropology.

From the biological side of anthropological studies, these further insights must be added:

9. Although the peoples of the world may be roughly (and arbitrarily) divided into different "races," or major groups, based on physical characteristics, there are no pure races, and probably never have been. There are large numbers of individuals who are intermediate in racial characteristics, so that no sharp "boundaries" can be drawn separating the "Negroid," "Caucasoid," and "Mongoloid" peoples.

10. There is no undisputed evidence of significant differences in ability or intelligence among major racial groupings of the world.

11. Contrary to beliefs still widely held, individuals who are the products of racial "mixing," or inter-breeding, are frequently superior to their "pure-blooded" parents in strength, stature, and other characteristics. This phenomenon of "hybrid vigor" is well known among many species of "lower" animals and plants as well.

12. Anthropologists (and other scientists) have discovered no human biological characteristics that are unaffected by life experiences and environmental conditions. Conversely, no human characteristics of thought or action can be regarded as unaffected by genetically inherited biological factors.

Anthropologists have frequently clashed with advocates of "white supremacy," "Aryan superiority," and other forms of racism. Such racists, from Count Gobineau a century ago down to Adolph Hitler and (currently) Carleton Putnam, have either ignored the anthropological evidence altogether or else grossly distorted those materials for their own prejudiced purposes. The central premise of anthropologists in opposition to the racists continues to be:

13. Practically all the significant differences in behavior among human populations (including expression of attitudes, "intelligence," and other psychological characteristics) are understandable as learned cultural patterns rather than biologically inherited characteristics.

MAJOR PROBLEMS FOR RESEARCH

Our inventory of the research achievements of anthropology actually represents only a bare initial framework for a science of human behavior. Each of the postulates listed above raises dozens of pertinent research questions. Detailed, precise knowledge that would effectively predict human cultural behavior under particular circumstances is still very far from realization. Anthropologists badly need more precise tools for observing, recording, and analyzing cultures.

A. *Methodological problems for research.*

1. Anthropological observation must be developed to adequately reflect the great variations in behavior found in even the simplest societies. Until recent times anthropologists have paid little attention to problems of "adequate samples" and representativeness of their data. It had been felt that the behavior of primitive people is so bound by custom that there is little variation, so that deviations from custom are readily recognizable. The impression of uniformity of behavior in simple societies is probably a distortion from reality produced by earlier anthropologists' overly simple research techniques and assumptions.

2. New and more culture-free psychological tests and other techniques need to be devised for cross-cultural study of motives, attitudes, values, intelligence, and other individual characteristics. Practically all the tests and devices now used were created for use among literate (often "middle-class") members of Western society, so there are serious problems of comparability of test results even in subgroups within American culture.

3. Anthropological field work must eliminate or at least minimize the effects of the emotional biases of the observer. (One way of partially achieving this goal is through team research, in which several observers with different points of view carry out field work in the same community.)

4. Standard units of observation or behavior that are equally applicable in a wide range of different cultures must be devised. Many of our earlier categories of observation (e.g., patrilocal residence, fertility rites, polytheism, hunting-and-gathering society) are rough-and-ready pigeonholes into which we place a rather mixed bag of actual behavior. More refined concepts are needed in practically all aspects of human behavior.

5. Theoretical constructs such as "acculturation," "individualism," "social disorganization," "cultural disorganization," "co-operation," "male dominance," and many others are badly in need of more refined operational definitions.

6. Anthropologists need to seek out more situations that approximate experimental conditions. For example, anthropologists

can occasionally find pairs (or larger groups) of societies which are culturally very much alike, *except* for some new, "experimental" change in one of the cases, the effects of which the anthropologist can compare with the situation in the society that did not experience the particular introduced change. Modern statistical methods offer the possibility that the anthropologist can observe and measure the differential effects of several variables simultaneously.

7. The relatively simple, face-to-face community study techniques of the anthropologist need to be modified and supplemented for study of complex, multi-community societies, including our own.

B. *Theoretical problems for research.*

As has been suggested above, the theoretical problems crying for research are so numerous that any listing seems pointless or distorted. However, here are some intriguing questions that have frequently haunted anthropologists:

1. To what extent is it possible (and likely) for societies to maintain diversity, even disagreement, on basic values and beliefs and still remain viable, "organized" social systems?

Earlier anthropological (and other social) theory laid great stress on the need for a society to have a consensus of values, or agreement on norms, in order to be healthy. More recently, there has been increasing logical and empirical evidence that such unanimity concerning major values and attitudes is not a *sine qua non* for interaction and cooperation even in simpler social systems.

2. To what extent is it possible (and likely) for peoples to change their beliefs and practices rapidly without suffering cultural disintegration and mental disorder?

Again, the earlier position of anthropologists has been that rapid culture change is inevitably disruptive and unhealthy. All cultures change, however, and most peoples in the world today are experiencing relatively rapid change. The great theoretical problem is: how much and what kinds of changes are "disruptive" and "mentally harmful?"

3. To what extent can similar types of developments in cultural evolution be found among the diverse environments and cultures in the world?

This is the question which the nineteenth-century evolutionists thought they had answered and to which modern anthropologists have now returned with renewed interest. (See discussion of multilinear evolution in Chapter 4, p. 59.)

4. To what extent, in terms of standards such as mental and physical health, can evaluations be made about some cultural patterns and systems being "better" or "healthier" than others?

Many anthropologists take the view that no absolute judgments can be made concerning the merits of different cultural patterns and systems. On the other hand, those in applied anthropology are engaged in numerous development programs where such cultural evaluations must be made. Billions of dollars are being spent by governments and private agencies in technical assistance, aid to "developing nations," and many other programs that are based on assumptions concerning relative "backwardness," "progress," and other value judgments. The intentions underlying these programs are in most cases quite laudable. But the value judgments involved in the application of these intentions to specific communities are most often left unexamined. Much of the most interesting new knowledge in applied anthropology is in the area of the "unintended consequences" of particular development projects.

Of course, the anthropologist's primary task is not evaluation of cultural patterns as "better" or "worse," for such normative judgments are often the main causes of subjective (and faulty) ethnographic observation. The most important work in anthropology will be in the building of theory in terms of which the varieties of human behavior can become more understandable and predictable. Without such understanding, well-intentioned programs of development and "modernization" can often result in much unintended cultural disorganization and human suffering among the people who are supposed to benefit from such programs.

SUMMARY AND CONCLUSIONS

Man's abilities to create and to manipulate systems of symbolic communication mark him off as distinct from other animals. The various symbol systems—the cultures—of different peoples can all be regarded as ways of adapting to particular environments. Cultural customs must be examined, therefore, in the total context of circumstances in which they occur. We have now accumulated a respectable inventory of cultural descriptions both past and present relating to different environments; an exciting new stage of anthropological study appears to be in the making.

Anthropology is often considered a collection of curious facts, telling about the peculiar appearance of exotic people and describing their strange customs and beliefs. It is looked upon as an entertaining diversion, apparently without bearing upon the conduct of life of civilized communities.

This opinion is mistaken. More than that, I hope to demonstrate that a clear understanding of the principles of anthropology illuminates the social processes of our own times and may show us, if we are ready to listen to its teaching, what to do and what to avoid.[7]

Suggested Reading

Goodenough, Ward. *Cooperation in Change.* New York: Russell Sage Foundation, 1963.

> Ward Goodenough, who has made significant contributions to both theoretical and applied anthropology, constructs a systematic framework of anthropological theory for application to programs of planned culture change.

Spicer, Edward A. (ed.). *Human Problems in Technological Change: A Casebook.* New York: Russell Sage Foundation, 1952.

> The focus of this casebook is on the cultural reasons for some unexpected problems in programs of technological change: why Eskimos are recalcitrant reindeer herders; why Spanish-Americans rejected an "improved" variety of corn; what happened when some Papago Indians acquired wagons for the first time; and several other interesting cases.

Tax, Sol (ed.). *Horizons of Anthropology.* Chicago: Aldine Publishing Company, 1964.

> This collection of papers was prepared for broadcast on a special Voice of America series. The anthropologists chosen for the project represent the younger generation of the discipline (most of them are in their thirties), and their excellent summary articles show that important new theoretical developments are taking place in anthropology.

---

[7] Franz Boas, *Anthropology and Modern Life* (New York: W. W. Norton and Co., 1928).

chapter six

Suggested Methods for Teachers

Raymond H. Muessig
and
Vincent R. Rogers

INTRODUCTION

Walter Goldschmidt has observed that "cultures are many, though man is one."[1] Goldschmidt's succinct observation is laden with meaning for many anthropologists. Yet this same statement would be a misty truism to numerous lay adults and most elementary and secondary school students. Whether similar expressions are viewed as self-evident or worthy of continued investigation depends a great deal on the cognitive and emotive background of the perceiver. Agronomic knowledge can make a difference in the yield Farmer Jones gets from an acre of ground. And the study of anthropology can increase what one gleans from its individual generalizations.

The preceding chapters have outlined a conceptual frame work which gives scholarly support to reflections like Goldschmidt's. This chapter extends that structure to include some ways of developing representative anthropological insights in our schools. We were impressed repeatedly with the many teachable ideas emerging naturally from Dr. Pelto's manuscript. However, we can concentrate upon only eight of them in this brief chapter.

*1. It Appears That Humans Everywhere Shape Their Beliefs
and Behavior in Response to the Same Fundamental
Human Problems and Needs.*

Apparently, there are certain basic problems that must be solved and needs that must be satisfied by people everywhere,

[1] *Exploring the Ways of Mankind* (New York: Holt, Rinehart & Winston, Inc., 1960), p. 12.

though their means of reaching solutions and achieving satisfactions may be different. Man gets hungry and must eat. He becomes tired and has to rest and sleep. He feels discomfort when confronted by unfriendly elements and seeks protection and shelter. He faces the mysteries of birth, life, and death, and procreates, nurtures his young, and ponders mortality and immortality. He sees the sun, moon, and stars and explains them in diverse ways.

An understanding of man's problems and needs and how he views them and deals with them in his various settings is a crucial aspect of the "anthropological point of view." Approaches such as those below might help children and youth see more clearly both the universality of man's plights, feelings, and wants and the directions from which he meets them.

Edward Steichen's magnificent photographic collection, *The Family of Man*,[2] could serve as one means of examining certain of man's distresses, labors, aspirations, and fulfillments. The pictorial format lends itself to convenient use at most levels of instruction. *The Family of Man* contains pictures dealing with a wide range of human experience from countries all over the world, including the United States, Italy, Germany, Sweden, Russia, China, India, the Congo, New Guinea, and many others. Pictures might be passed around the classroom, held up in front of the class, shown on an opaque projector, or displayed in mounted form on a bulletin board. Initially, students might view a few pictures relevant to a single motif until they capture Steichen's intent. Younger pupils might discuss photographs of children playing in different areas. Older students might respond to various forms of work or wedding ceremonies. Next, illustrations clustered around themes pertinent to emotion or maturation might be employed. Later, the teacher could ask the class to originate titles for the entire exhibit and compare their ideas with the original title. Eventually, students might frame an over-all generalization suggested by Steichen's compilation which would be similar to the one under discussion here.

Another visual avenue to a consideration of humankind's rudimentary difficulties, necessities, and challenges involves the use of young people's drawings and paintings from other parts of the world. Collections may be borrowed from agencies such as the Asia Society and the Japan Society. An inexpensive source is the annual children's art competition edition of *Shankar's Weekly*,

2 New York: Maco Magazine Corporation, 1955.

the Indian magazine published in New Delhi. Apparel and settings differ, of course, from culture to culture, but the subject matter of children's drawings is often strikingly similar. For example, food, clothing, and shelter needs and parent-child relationships often appear.

Hans Reich's collection of photographs entitled *Children of Many Lands*[3] can be used in a slightly different fashion to help youngsters grasp the first major understanding we have identified in this chapter. The teacher might choose a number of pictures of the world's children, captured in certain moods and engaged in various activities. At first, the class might be asked to look for all the *differences* apparent in the photographs. Perhaps the children would become somewhat preoccupied with dress and other more superficial points. Then, having enumerated differences, they could be encouraged to probe for similarities.

Even very young children can come up with a few human similarities through the use of stories such as *Tommy and Dee-Dee*. This book is a simply written and cleverly illustrated comparison of Tommy, an American five-year-old, and Dee-Dee, his Chinese counterpart. The first half of the book emphasizes all sorts of differences between the two children. The kindergarten or first grade teacher might pause at the halfway point to invite comments and questions. Following the reading of the second half of *Tommy and Dee-Dee*, the teacher might use these excerpts (with their accompanying pictures, of course) as the basis for an explicit discussion of some shared reactions:

But
Tommy loves candy.
Dee-Dee loves candy, too.

Tommy likes to play cowboy hunting a bad man.
Dee-Dee likes to play chasing a bad man on a horse, too.

Dee-Dee loves parades.
Tommy loves parades, too.

When Tommy is hurt, he goes "Wah-wah."
When Dee-Dee cries, she goes "Wah-wah," too.

When they laugh, both say "Ha-ha, ha-ha!"
They live half a world apart, but aren't they a lot alike? [4]

---

[3] New York: Hill & Wang, Inc., 1958.
[4] Yen Liang, *Tommy and Dee-Dee* (New York: Henry Z. Walck, Inc., 1953), pp. 15–29.

"Some Children Are . . .," a poem by Jo Tenjford of Oslo, Norway,[5] could be used in the intermediate grades to pursue our initial anthropological insight:

Some children are brown
  like newly baked bread,
some children are yellow
  and some are red,
some children are white
  and some almost blue
Their colors are different—
  the children like you!

Some children eat porridge
  and some eat figs,
some children like ice-cream
  and some roasted pigs!
Some eat raw fishes
  and some Irish stew—
Their likings are different—
  the children like you!

Some children say "yes"
  and some say "oui"
some say "ja"
  and some say "si,"
some children say "peep,"
  and some say "booh—"
Their words may be different—
  the children like you!

Some children wear sweaters
  and some rebozos,
some children wear furs
  and some kimonos,
some children go naked
  and wear only their queue.
Their clothes may be different—
  the children like you!

Some children have houses
  of stone in the streets,
some live in igloos,
  and some live on fleets.
Some live in old strawhuts
  and some in new—

---

[5] Distributed by the National Conference of Christians and Jews, Inc., 43 West 57th Street, New York, New York, 10019.

Their homes may be different—
the children like you!

Some children are Finnish
and some from Japan,
some are Norwegian
and some from Sudan.
Oh yes, we have children
in valley, on pike.
Their countries are different—
the children alike!

Oh, if they could dance
and if they could play
altogether together
a wonderful day!
Some could come sailing
and some could just hike!
So much would be different—
the children alike!

Another possibility would be for the teacher to read to his class three or four cross-cultural explanations of the earth's creation and the beginning of man as described in Sophia Fahs' fascinating book, *Beginnings: Earth, Sky, Life, and Death.*[6] Fahs includes, for example, the Australian aborigine legend about the first sunrise and sunset; the Iroquois Indian story of the first animals; a Miwok Indian myth about man's origins; and many others. The teacher could gear his discussion to the idea that there are certain persisting questions that all societies have asked from time immemorial. The answers arrived at have varied, but the questions have been the same.

Finally, in a similar vein, senior high school students could profit from reading Pearl Buck's beautiful story, *The Big Wave.* It concerns a Japanese family living in an area threatened by a tidal wave. When a child expresses a fear of the wave and of death itself, his father offers this explanation:

"Death is a great gateway," Kino's father said.
His face was not at all sad. Instead, it was quiet and happy.

"The gateway—where?" Kino asked again.

Kino's father smiled. "Can you remember when you were born?"

Kino shook his head. "I was too small."

---

[6] Boston: Beacon Press, 1960.

Kino's father laughed. "I remember very well. Oh, how hard you thought it was to be born! You cried and you screamed."

"Didn't I want to be born?" Kino asked. This was very interesting to him.

"You did not," his father told him smiling. "You wanted to stay just where you were in the warm, dark house of the unborn. But the time came to be born, and the gate of life opened."

"Did I know it was the gate of life?" Kino asked.

"You did not know anything about it and so you were afraid of it," his father replied. "But see how foolish you were! Here we were waiting for you, your parents, already loving you and eager to welcome you. And you have been very happy, haven't you?"

"Until the big wave came," Kino replied. "Now I am afraid again because of the death that the big wave brought."

"You are only afraid because you don't know anything about death," his father replied. "But someday you will wonder why you were afraid, even as today you wonder why you feared to be born."[7]

Again, the class might discuss the Japanese father's explanation, compare it with others reported in factual and fictional sources, and enlarge upon points brought out. Ultimately, the teacher could guide students to the realization that people everywhere have had to face death and have attempted to frame answers concerned with its meaning.

2. *Practically All Important Differences in Human Behavior Are Understandable as Variations in Learned Patterns of Social Behavior—Not Differences in Biological Apparatus, Type of Blood, or Any Other Genetically Inherited Mechanism.*

In our diverse world, children and youth must understand that man's biological inheritance permits myriad forms of behavior. It also sets certain limitations on the things he can do. Man can learn a language or languages, recall past events, think and record his reflections. He cannot remain under water for extended lengths of time without special equipment he has invented, endure a subzero temperature or be exposed a long time to the rays of a

---

[7] Copyright © 1948. Reprinted from *The Big Wave*, pp. 36–37, by Pearl S. Buck. By permission of the John Day Company, Inc., publisher.

blazing sun without any protective clothing or shelter, or crush a boulder with his bare hands. Man has created and adjusted to a seemingly endless variety of cultures—born out of the necessity to satisfy biological demands but also possessing attributes that have transcended purely physiological factors. Man's biological structure makes it possible for him to see, hear, smell, taste, and feel. His culture can affect the forms, shapes, and colors he perceives, likes, or dislikes; the sounds he finds pleasant, unpleasant, reassuring, or frightening; the smells and tastes that he savors or avoids; and the tactile sensations that he finds comfortable or uncomfortable. His body can be developed so that it possesses sufficient strength to kill an adversary or to tow a drowning man from a lake. The potential power of the body is biological; its use is socially learned and reinforced.

There are many ways a classroom teacher could approach our second generalization. Subject to the maturity of his students, he could concentrate on one or a group of the basic biological senses and needs. For example, he might ask class members to comb through magazines and newspapers at home and to bring all of the pictures they can find that show babies, children, young adults, and adults sleeping in different parts of the world. After a student committee has prepared a bulletin board display of the illustrations, the teacher might ask, or write on the chalk board for purposes of discussion (or for independent study and written response), questions such as these:

Do people all over the world have to sleep? Why or why not? How do you know your answer is right?
Do all people sleep in beds? Why or why not?
Do all people sleep at night as you do? Why or why not?
Do all people sleep the same amount of time? Why or why not?

Pupils would observe that every person has to sleep because his biological make-up demands it. They could discover, however, that where and when he sleeps and how much sleep he gets can be influenced by his culture. For instance, they might point out that babies sleep in their mothers' arms, various carrying devices, buggies, packed straw, baskets, hammocks, cribs, beds, and so on. They would find that a person's occupation can determine when he sleeps. Shift workers, palace guards, policemen, night cleaning ladies and waitresses, and many others work while members of the class are in bed. Pupils may realize that medical doctors

working during disasters, soldiers engaged in battle, farmers harvesting wheat, and college students studying for final examinations may go without sleep for prolonged periods of time or get by with only "cat naps."

During a discussion of man's basic needs and functions, senior high school students might identify the sex drive and recognize the importance of procreation as a *sine qua non* in human survival. Little direction and time would be required for them to discover also that culture may influence the age marriage is encouraged, permitted, or considered feasible, the choice of a mate or the arrangements of a marriage contract between families, the duration of a marriage, and so on. Using a statistical or demographic source, students may observe easily the difference in the age of persons getting married in different cultures. They could compare India and Ireland, for example. Interesting questions should emerge as students attempt to explain such phenomena. They would surely find that much of man's behavior cannot be explained solely on the basis of his biological properties.

The senses of sight, hearing, smell, and taste can be explored easily with respect to their cultural connotations. In a factory or store close to the school, pupils might observe an inspector, foreman, technician, or clerk whose eyes have been trained to detect the slightest imperfections in products that might pass unseen by others. Similarly, children could watch a piano tuner adjust the pitch of a school piano, noting the developed sensitivity of his hearing.

The same technique could be used to illustrate how the sense of smell can be culturally adjusted. People residing near a slaughtering plant, a paper mill, or an aluminum plant may become unaware eventually of an odor that was once stifling for them. A clerk at a perfume counter can identify many brands by their aroma, something she could not do when she first accepted the job. Soldiers are taught to smell various types of poison gas. And many American consumers are completely intoxicated by the combined metal, rubber, cloth, and paint aromas that tell them they are sitting in a *new* automobile!

Children can also perceive cultural factors attached to the biological sense of taste. To investigate this area, the teacher could make a check list of domestic and foreign foods, asking each pupil to indicate flavors he enjoys. Or, the teacher could serve a dish with a distinctive flavor (heavily spiced, very sweet or sour, etc.) and invite reactions. Pupils would probably see that they have

learned to like many foods as a result of their exposure to them. Eventually, they might observe that they doubtless could have learned or could still learn to appreciate many kinds of foods and flavors if presented with continual opportunity.

Taking a different tack, the teacher could study with his pupils what is now known about obvious biological properties such as skin, hair, and eye color; hair texture; nose and head shape; and blood type. Content and materials could be adjusted quite easily to the age and ability level of the class. For instance, Marguerite Rush Lerner, a medical doctor, has written a brotherhood-award-winning children's book entitled *Red Man, White Man, African Chief: The Story of Skin Color*[8] which some second-graders, a number of third-graders, and most fourth-graders can read and understand. Lerner discusses pigmentation in general, pointing out that all things, such as carrots, contain a coloring agent. The book leads gradually into the idea that all human beings have melanin (the main pigment in skin, hair, and eyes) in their skin and that its state of dispersion or scattering determines how dark a person appears.

On a more advanced level, senior high school students could read and discuss *The Races of Mankind*.[9] This brief, meaningfully illustrated pamphlet states that the peoples of the earth have a common origin. It suggests that all races of men can "either plow or fight" and that racial differences among them do not explain their behavior. It handles racial characteristics, height, brain size, and blood type in a matter-of-fact manner, pointing out that experience, environment, and opportunity are the crucial factors in social behavior. High-ability senior high school students might tackle *Heredity, Race and Society*, written by two zoologists, L. C. Dunn and Theodosius Dobzhansky,[10] and available in paperback form. Dunn and Dobzhansky examine human differences from a scientific frame of reference and draw some helpful distinctions between biological and cultural factors. Any number of publications like these could be employed to develop important ideas. An early understanding of these ideas might do a great deal to modify, if not completely change, some beliefs erroneously held by many Americans.

---

[8] Minneapolis: Lerner Publications Co., 1960.

[9] By Ruth Benedict and Gene Weltfish (New York: Public Affairs Pamphlets, 1951).

[10] Mentor Books edition, revised and enlarged; New York: New American Library of World Literature, Inc., 1957.

3. *Every Society Has Regular Patterns of Behavior That Make It Possible for Individuals to Predict Each Other's Behavior and to Act Accordingly.*

Rarely do people behave in a completely random manner. As they attempt to satisfy their needs, their behavior is goal-directed. They have learned to count on some degree of consistency in their culture so they can project the possible consequences of their actions and their interactions with others. A sense of stability and security is provided by the knowledge that certain forms of behavior are repetitive or duplicative. Children and youth direct many things they say and do by anticipating outcomes. They can learn that the anthropologist searches for underlying principles of cultural and social systems through the study of a wide range of human ways of living.

The more samples of human behavior the anthropologist can gather, the better he can formulate valid and reliable generalizations and make accurate predictions. These anthropological generalizations and predictions have influenced and will continue to shape some of man's decisions regarding human needs, aspirations, and relationships.

There are numerous ways of exposing children in the primary grades to the idea that elements of human behavior can be observed, recorded, and then predicted. The teacher might initiate the exposure by saying something like this:

> Can you pretend today that each of you is the only one in our group who is absent from school because of a bad cold? Make believe that it is not quite time for school to start and that you are in bed thinking of what the rest of the children will be doing all day. Let's begin with the "Pledge of Allegiance" as the first thing on our list. Now, what might happen next?

The teacher would write on the chalkboard each of the hypothetical day's activities in sequence as recalled and suggested by the class. Next, the children would discuss how they knew the order of events that would probably take place. The youngsters could be asked then to give other examples of things familiar to them outside of school that fall into a persistent, reliable developmental pattern. For instance, each child with a younger brother or sister could be helped to compose a step-by-step, numbered list of the things that usually happen around the little one's bedtime.

The teacher could also ask the class to identify a few examples of misbehavior involving children their age that occur frequently in the immediate community and to predict how local parents might handle these minor disciplinary problems. Following this discussion of anticipated parental behavior, the teacher might describe a situation in which a Hopi Indian child, for example, does something "wrong." Again, the class would be invited to predict what might happen. Next, the teacher could read a passage from Bernadine Beatie's "Little Turtle"[11] in which a Hopi youngster is punished *not* by his father but by his mother's brother. The teacher could add that the uncle's action does not surprise the Hopi boy. Rather, it is what he has come to expect. Using the Hopi instance and other illustrations, the teacher could help the class discover that much of what an individual learns to anticipate in given situations is a product of repeated instances within a given cultural framework. The children might try also to imagine what it would be like to be dropped abruptly into a strange land where everything was so different that one could not know what he should do nor predict how others might react to his behavior. Portions of books such as Lewis Carroll's *Alice's Adventures in Wonderland* and Jonathan Swift's *Gulliver's Travels* convey this feeling and might be read to the children.

Another possibility for dealing with our third major anthropological insight could be used at a variety of grade levels. Each pupil would be given a duplicated inventory of objects and instructed to put a *B* for *boy* and a *G* for *girl* in front of the thing they think a boy or girl might play with, wear, etc. Items on the list could be tailor-made to the age level of the class. A portion of the form might look like this:

.... football helmet	.... jump rope	.... purse
.... party dress	.... model car	.... baseball
.... hair ribbon	.... bracelet	.... pet snake

The teacher would then copy the items on the chalkboard, putting *B* and *G* columns in front of them so the students' responses could be tabulated in their presence. If items were carefully chosen,

[11] In *Jack and Jill*, XXIV, No. 10 (August 1962), 2–7.

the choices would be fairly clear cut. Next, the teacher could take a given object and ask a series of questions. He might begin with, "Why did all of you put a *G* in front of 'party dress?'" The group might reply that only *girls* wear dresses! The teacher could follow this response with, "Don't boys *ever* wear dresses?" He would probably be assured that this is the case. Then he might ask, "Why is this so?" The class could say a number of things here, many of which might boil down to "Just because it's the *right* thing to do." The teacher could enlarge this discussion until the students perceived that the wearing of dresses by American girls is a common custom that is taken for granted and passed on from year to year. Americans can predict that girls will be wearing dresses tomorrow and next week when they come to school. Clothing manufacturers, stores, clerks, parents, children, and others all make this assumption.

Having established the regularity of the wearing of dresses as a behavioral pattern, the teacher could point out some exceptions and cultural differences. He could ask whether girls *always* wear dresses in the United States. The class would realize almost immediately that girls wear overalls, slacks, pedal pushers, shorts, bathing suits, and so on—depending on the situation. The teacher might then query, "But you said that boys and men *never have* and *never do* wear dresses in the United States or *anywhere else,* right?" Eventually, he could show the class photographs of American baby boys in their christening dresses, Scotsmen wearing kilts, Greek soldiers in World War II wearing their traditional ceremonial "skirts," and men sporting beautiful wrap-around "skirts" on various South Sea islands. The class should get some introduction to the idea that what is "right" in dress, as in many other things, is culturally defined and predictable only if one knows a great deal about the culture.

Appropriate to their maturation level, students ranging from the fifth through the twelfth grades might be read a passage describing a child or an adult placed in a difficult problem situation, faced with a crucial dilemma, or confronted with a serious moral decision. Without suggesting any cultural, societal, geographical, or chronological context, the teacher would invite a class discussion in which students would *predict* what the individual *will do.* In most instances, the students would respond in terms of their own frame of reference, setting, and time. Then, the teacher would give each student a slip of paper on which is specified the identity of the person, what his position and status are in a given society, when the action is taking place, and where the situation is occurring. The "how" is left up to the student. After reading to fill in the background necessary for an informed response, he predicts how the individual will behave. The entire class then shares the results of independent study and research. Some students may observe that they were unable to find sufficient data upon which to build an accurate prognosis. (If this occurs, the students should be praised publicly for their recognition of the necessity to reserve judgment; and the teacher should feel that this is one of the great days in his career!) Other students may have done a great deal of work and may feel that a tentative prediction is in order. They would be expected to defend with facts the projection of behavior they have made.

After individual reports have been made and discussed in class, the teacher could draw a horizontal line across the chalkboard and challenge the class to place tentative predictions of behavior along this line according to degrees of similarity or dissimilarity, importance or lack of importance, or some other criterion in given cultural settings. Below are two very brief illustrations of the kinds of passages teachers might read to their students to stimulate this activity:

> Some boys are playing together. One boy says that they should have a race. Another boy, who is smaller than the rest, states that he does not want to run in the race. He starts to walk slowly away from the others, but he is stopped by the boy who suggested the race. What will happen next?

> A handsome young man works in a place where he sees a beautiful young lady almost every day. He is strong, healthy, and intelligent. He does not have a wife. He would like to be married and to have a family. The young lady is graceful, well mannered, and charming. She too is unmarried. What will happen next?

The teacher might eventually point out that the group of boys were Hopi Indians, among whom competition of any kind is frowned upon. Perhaps the boy-girl story might involve a higher caste girl from India being admired by a lower caste boy a century ago. In either case, the class should understand that predicting behavior is almost impossible unless one is familiar with the lifeways of the group in question.

4. Man's Perceptions of His Experiences Are Strongly Influenced by His Cultural Heritage; and He Tends to View His Own Way of Life as the Most Reasonable and Natural.

No human being has a completely neutral, objective approach to this heterogeneous world of ours. As Ruth Benedict put it, "The lenses through which any nation looks at life are not the ones that other nations use."[12] Man's experiences and emotions develop within a particular context. When he tries to enter the unique frame of reference of another individual or group, he cannot check his own cultural heritage at the door as he might deposit his hat and coat with a restaurant checkroom attendant. Yet this is no reason for assuming that children at *all* grade levels cannot examine other people's lifeways with both understanding and empathy. Franz Boas' distinction between viewing one's own culture as "higher" than others and viewing it as "dearer" to oneself than others is vital if one aspires to the "anthropological point of view."[13] Children and youth in our elementary and secondary schools can have many opportunities to study peoples who live and have lived in other parts of the globe. Whether or not these students emerge from their classrooms even more ethnocentric than when they began their education may depend largely upon each teacher's content emphases, methodological approaches, and personal characteristics.

Many techniques may be evolved by teachers to help their charges realize that an individual's cultural matrix can affect how he responds to a given stimulus object or situation. For instance, the teacher might ask a group of children to write their thoughts about the story behind a particular picture. Perhaps he would show his class a picture of a new bicycle. He could ask the class to guess who would own the bike and how it would be used. Many children might write about a boy who will receive the bicycle for his birthday and use it to ride to school, to go places with his friends, to get groceries for his mother, to deliver papers, and so forth. Then, the class might be told that an elderly gentleman had purchased it to get some exercise. The teacher could help his pupils see that they had looked at the situation entirely in terms of their own personal experience.

---

[12] In *The Chrysanthemum and the Sword* (Boston: Houghton Mifflin Co., 1946), p. 14.
[13] Franz Boas, *The Mind of Primitive Man* (New York: The Macmillan Co., 1938), p. 225.

The old Russian folk tale, *My Mother Is the Most Beautiful Woman in the World*, offers another approach to the fourth anthropological generalization we have drawn from Professor Pelto's manuscript. The story concerns a little girl, Varya, who is lost. She tells some friendly villagers who are trying to help find her mother that her mother is "the most beautiful woman in the world!" One by one, the prettiest women are sought, but still Varya's mother is not found. Finally, the story concludes with this passage:

> Just then a breathless, excited woman came puffing up to the crowd. Her face was big and broad, and her body even larger. Her eyes were little pale slits between a great lump of a nose. The mouth was almost toothless. Even as a young girl everyone had said, "A homely girl like Marfa is lucky to get a good husband like Ivan."
>
> "Varyachka!" cried this woman.
>
> "Mamochka!" cried the little girl, and they fell into each other's arms. The two of them beamed upon each other. Varya cuddled into the ample and familiar bosom. The smile Varya had longed for was once again shining upon her.
>
> All of the villagers smiled thankfully when Varya looked up from her mother's shoulder and said with joy: "This is my mother! I told you my mother is the most beautiful woman in the world!"[14]

The children would then be asked to discuss at some length the reasons for Varya's description of her mother. They might agree finally with the revelation implied in the story that some people may appear beautiful to us because we love them.

The book, *Anna and the King of Siam*, which inspired the familiar musical *The King and I*, is laden with methodological possibilities relevant to our fourth insight. The following excerpt speaks for itself:

> Then a slave crouched down in front of Anna and pointed at the English woman's nose. She wanted to know, it seemed, whether Anna's nose had grown long from much pulling, and also whether it had to be arranged every morning to keep it so. Anna assured her that the size of the nose was not a matter of exercise or volition on the part of its owner, but a work of nature. The slave clucked in sympathy and turned away fingering her own flat nose gratefully.[15]

---

[14] By permission of Lothrop, Lee & Shepard Co., Inc., from *My Mother Is the Most Beautiful Woman in the World*, p. 28, by Becky Rehyer; © 1945 by Becky Rehyer and Ruth Gannett.

[15] Copyright © 1943, 1944 by Margaret Mortenson Landon. Reprinted from *Anna and the King of Siam*, p. 97, by Margaret Mortenson Landon. By permission of The John Day Company, Inc., publisher.

As older students discuss the American Revolution, the teacher might have them listen carefully to a statement made by the British general, John Burgoyne, who often complained bitterly about American methods of fighting. Here he describes what to him seemed like the most unsoldierly conduct:

> . . . the country [is] full of woods, swamps, stone walls and other hiding places. It may be said of it that every man will, in action, turn every tree and bush into a kind of temporary fortress . . .[16]

At this point, the teacher could invite the class to discuss why Burgoyne held certain expectations about "accepted" ways of fighting and why he felt American military tactics were "unfair" and "ungentlemanly."

Helping students to see themselves as others see them appears to be a useful and effective way to soften portions of the ethnocentric shell. One procedure might be built around the selection below which could be read aloud to the class or reproduced so each student would have his own copy. The teacher would introduce the passage as an anthropologist's description of the practices of a tribe called the Nacirema.

> The focal point of the shrine is a box or chest which is built into the wall. In this chest are kept the many charms and magical potions without which no native believes he could live . . . The charm is not disposed of after it has served its purpose, but is placed in the charm-box of the household shrine. As these magical materials are specific for certain ills, and the real or imagined maladies of the people are many, the charm-box is usually full to overflowing. The magical packets are so numerous that people forget what their purposes were and fear to use them again. While the natives are very vague on this point, we can only assume that the idea in retaining all the old magical materials is that their presence in the charm-box will in some way protect the worshipper.[17]

Then the teacher could ask questions such as the following about the Nacirema:

> Do you approve or disapprove of the Nacirema? Why or why not?

---

[16] Marshall D. Davidson, *Life in America* (Boston: Houghton Mifflin Co., 1951), p. 144.

[17] Horace Miner, "Body Ritual Among the Nacirema," *American Anthropologist*, LVIII, No. 3 (June 1956), 504.

Do their practices make sense to you?

Have you ever heard of any other group which follows similar practices?

Does anyone know who the Nacirema really are?

If the class does not guess who these people are, the teacher would tell them that "Nacirema" is really American spelled backward. The description, of course, is of a typical American bathroom medicine chest. Next, the class might discuss briefly other forms of behavior in the United States that seem reasonable and natural to Americans which might be viewed in other ways by people living in different countries and *vice versa*. Again, the "why" of this phenomenon, as with others, should be analyzed.

Language differences offer another opportunity for the creative teacher to help students react sympathetically to the actions of others. For example, the teacher might review the story of Lerner and Loewe's *My Fair Lady,* based upon George Bernard Shaw's *Pygmalion.* Carefully chosen portions from the original cast recording should be played in class, particularly the song "Why Can't the English?" which Henry Higgins sings after hearing Eliza Doolittle speak. The class might then discuss the reactions of the English gentleman to cockney speech patterns. Questions like these might be explored:

How do you suppose Eliza sounded to Henry?

How did she react to his way of speaking?

How do both Eliza and Henry sound to you?

Which of the two is "right?"

How might Eliza's friends react when they heard her new way of speaking? Would they think Eliza's speech had "improved?"

The class interaction might be continued by referring to some speech patterns one is likely to hear in the United States. For instance, the teacher could raise a question about the New Englander's tendency to drop the *r* from words like "car" or "barn." The class might be asked whether the New England "accent" is "right" or "wrong." They might reflect on how they have reacted in the past when they have heard speech patterns different from their own. They could also tape-record some of their conversation and listen attentively for a possible accent peculiar to *their* physical location.

As a follow-up to this kind of discussion, the following passages from Lois Lenski's *Shoo-Fly Girl* might be read and discussed. Suzanna has been asked to spend her first night in a non-Amish home . . .

> Shoo-Fly went in Betty's house and looked around. It was very different from an Amish home. She stared with big eyes. There was so much to see.
>
> The rooms were small and very crowded. There were lace curtains and soft carpets and pictures on the wall, and books and magazines and framed photographs looking at you from every direction. Also, there was noise—the TV and a radio were blaring, and there was a piano to play . . . The telephone began to ring and kept on ringing . . . The whole house was an assault on her eyes and her ears.
>
> "What do you want to do?" Betty asked.
>
> "I don't know," said Shoo-Fly.
>
> "Let's look at TV," said Betty.
>
> They squatted on cushions on the floor and looked at the flickering screen. Shoo-Fly could see shadows like people darting back and forth, and she heard loud shouting noises. But she could not tell what it was all about. Then men began pointing guns and banging. It confused, then alarmed her.
>
> The telephone rang and Betty got up to answer it. Shoo-Fly listened to the one-sided conversation. She had never talked on the telephone in her life.
>
> Mrs. Ferguson had supper ready and Betty placed a chair for her. She folded her own hands in her lap to pray, but they began eating at once.
>
> Shoo-Fly took a few mouthfuls. Why had she come? She put down her fork. She tried hard not to cry. "I want to go home," she said.[18]

As a means of helping senior high school students examine man's tendency to view his own way of life as the most reasonable and natural, the teacher might initiate a general discussion dealing with commonly held American views of dating, courtship, and marriage. Students would doubtless reflect many romanticized ideas perpetuated by the media of mass communication centered around "getting a date," "going steady," falling in love," "popping the question," "being married," and "living happily ever after in a dream house." Students' answers to questions such as "Who does the asking when a date is desired or a marriage partner sought?"

---

[18] Lois Lenski, *Shoo-Fly Girl* (New York: J. B. Lippincott Co., 1963), pp. 87–88.

or "Who decides whether a couple will marry?" should bring out various culturally influenced perceptions about this facet of American life. Gradually, the teacher might ask what students would think of having their marriages arranged for them. Following a thorough expression of opinion, the teacher could introduce this report of a conversation that took place between an American educator and a group of teen-age girls in India:

"Wouldn't you like to be free to choose your own marriage partner?" I asked. "Oh, no!" several voices replied in chorus. I was taken aback. "Why not?" I asked.

"Doesn't it put the girl in a very humiliating position?" one girl said. . . . "Doesn't she have to try to look pretty, and call attention to herself, and attract a boy, to be sure she'll get married? . . . And if she doesn't want to do that or if she feels it's undignified, wouldn't that mean she mightn't get a husband? . . . Well, surely that's humiliating. It makes getting married a competition, in which girls fight each other for the boys. And it encourages a girl to pretend she's better than she really is. She has to make a good impression to get him to marry her. . . . In our system, we girls don't have to worry at all. We *know* we'll get married. When we are old enough, our parents find a suitable boy, and everything is arranged. . . . How could we judge the character of a boy we met? We are young and inexperienced. Our parents are older and wiser, and they aren't as easily deceived as we would be. I'd far rather have my parents choose for me. It's important that the man I marry is the right one. I could easily make a mistake if I had to select him myself."[19]

5. *Every Human Cultural System Is Logical and Coherent in Its Own Terms, Given the Basic Assumptions and Knowledge Available to the Specific Community.*

Franz Boas, in his classic study, *The Mind of Primitive Man*, concluded that "other things being equal, a race is commonly described as the lower, the more fundamentally it differs from our own."[20] The phenomenon Boas described can be attributed often to an individual's inability or unwillingness to examine the behavior of others in the light of what *they* know and believe. Viewing other's actions through his own contextual telescope, he is all too willing to label what he sees as "unusual," "odd," "stupid," or "wrong." It seems of utmost importance to us, then, that teachers

[19] David Mace, "Marriage by Arrangement," *McCalls*, XXCVI, No. 11 (August 1959), 50–51.
[20] *Op. cit.*, p. 5.

do all they can to help children and youth fathom the compelling relationship existing between the behavior of a group and their prime understandings and values.

Children could be moved toward this insight from anthropology by responding to a group of hypothetical situations. For example, they might imagine that they live in a village where there has been a long drought and where it is believed that rain can be caused by a very loud noise. Since rain is so badly needed, a contest will be held and a feast given in honor of the villager who can make the loudest noise. The teacher would instruct the youngsters to free their imaginations and tell what they might do if they were members of this society. Or, pupils might be asked to discuss or write about what they might do if they were to reside in a place where doing nice things for others is regarded as the most important thing in life. In every situation proposed, children would be requested to assess the behavior they have imagined with respect to the beliefs or values of the fictitious group.

To approach this generalization differently, a teacher might show his class three or four pictures of snow. One might show a driving blizzard, another a gentle snowfall, and still another packed snow on a sidewalk. He would ask the class what they see in each picture and help them note that the word "snow" was used in each reply. Then, he could write the following words on the chalkboard:

apingaut
sitidlorak
akelrorak
mauyak

The teacher would ask the class to guess what these words mean. He could then write the appropriate translation next to each word:

apingaut—first snowfall of the season
sitidlorak—hard, packed snow
akelrorak—newly drifted snow
mauyak—soft snow

At first, pupils might comment that those are "funny" words for "snow" and that it seems "silly" to have so many words for the same thing. At this point, the teacher might ask his charges if they have any idea what group of people might *need* and *use* a variety of words for "snow." Eskimos would be mentioned almost immediately. Following a brief dialogue on Eskimos and their environment, it would be apparent that precise definitions of types of snow might be a life or death matter. Next, the teacher might ask the children whether there could ever be a time when people *they* know would be interested in the kind of snow that has fallen. Pupils might respond that people who have to drive longer distances in the winter may be quite concerned with snow conditions. There is a big difference between rapidly melting, slushy snow and snow that is packed and icy! Or, pupils may observe that skiers head for the mountains on winter weekends when they hear that a fresh, powder snow is anticipated. With help, children could discover that "who," "when," and "where" factors can be directly relevant to the understanding of, interest in, importance of, or acceptance of many objects, functions, ideas, and commitments.

Students from the intermediate through the senior high school levels might be exposed to this generalization through an individualized "Can you make it make sense?" assignment. According to the grade level and the estimated ability of each student, the teacher would prepare brief descriptions of a number of human activities. On a 3" x 5" card, every class member would receive his own statement to consider, investigate, clarify, and later explain to his classmates. Many resources, written at various reading levels, would be brought into the classroom for this project. Adequate supervised study time and teacher assistance would be provided. Some students would be released to work in the school library. Older students might be encouraged to work in main municipal or university libraries or with scholars in accessible institutions of higher learning, if this is possible.

At first, each activity may appear to the student to have a "strange" cast to it. Initially, it may seem to be rather different or inexplicable on the one hand, or illogical, incoherent, impractical, unbelievable, or mysterious on the other. The student's task is to "make sense" out of the behavior, practice, custom, or belief by placing it as faithfully as he can in its cultural milieu.

The following is an example of what the teacher might put on one of the 3" x 5" cards:

CAN YOU MAKE IT MAKE SENSE?

For: Wayne Jenkins

At Delphi the ancient Greeks built a temple over a yellow vapor, believed to be the breath of the god Apollo, which came through a crack in the rocks. A woman oracle sat over the vapor in a drugged condition. It was thought that the words she mumbled were spoken by Apollo, and important persons from all over the Mediterranean area came to get her advice. The words of the prophetess could be understood only by priests. Answers to questions were put in a form that was almost impossible to prove wrong.

Other cards might deal with topics such as these:

A Northwest Indian potlatch ceremony in which an Indian chief burns his own canoes and destroys many other prized possessions in order to "defeat" a rival.

An Aztec, Mayan, or Inca ceremony involving human sacrifice.

A group that buries food, clothing, weapons, etc. with a dead warrior.

A tomb erected in memory of an unknown soldier.

A man who purchases a new car every year, even though his last car still runs perfectly.

A woman who sleeps on painful hair curlers all night long.

6. *Man Has the Capacity to Adopt, Adapt, and Reconstitute Present and Past Ideas, Beliefs, and Inventions of Others Who Are Living or Dead.*

"Man has no nature; he has history." Ortega y Gasset's observation, though overstated, seems fundamentally sound. There is no society, no culture, no people that has not been influenced in some way by the ideas of others. Anthropologists have gathered unmistakable evidence of the sharing of cultural elements "from tribe to tribe, from people to people and from continent to continent,"[21] as Boas put it. Indeed, the distinctive feature that makes man so different from other animals is that his lifeways are based on socially learned patterns of behavior. Other animals may have some rudiments of culture, but for man all social behavior is cultural.

Any society one might choose to study, then, engages in some forms of behavior that have been distilled from the past and borrowed from others. Furthermore, the process of cultural learning, adaptation, and synthesis goes on through time in a continuing procession. With ever emerging technological developments and improvements, man may expect the diffusion of ideas to increase.

21 *Op. cit.*, p. 168.

The teacher might move a class toward our sixth anthropological understanding through the use of language. While we speak the "English" language, a brief examination of a few commonly used words should indicate quite clearly that many of our words have been plucked from other cultures. The teacher could, for example, list this series of words on the chalkboard:

alligator	depot	oasis
boss	egg	tattoo
canoe	giraffe	tea
dachshund	kimono	toboggan
dandelion	kindergarten	wagon

The teacher might then ask the class to identify only the *English* words on the board, being sure to eliminate any words taken from other languages. There might be some discussion and even some disagreement, but the class would probably agree on a smaller group of words. Next, the teacher would challenge pupils to determine the derivation of each word labeled as English, "just to make sure." Eventually, the class would find that there were no "purebred" English words in the list. "Alligator," for example, is Spanish, "boss" Dutch, "canoe" Indian, "dandelion" French, "egg" Scandinavian, "giraffe" Arabic, "kimono" Japanese, "kindergarten" German, "oasis" Egyptian, "tattoo" Polynesian, and "tea" Chinese.

Students might then be asked to search out other examples of things familiar to them that have been borrowed or adapted from other cultures. Young children might discover that some of their favorite stories such as *Hansel and Gretel, Stone Soup, The Just So Stories,* and *The Ugly Duckling* were written in other countries. Youngsters in the intermediate grades could trace the origins of a group of our most beloved melodies, such as "Silent Night," "The Waltz of the Flowers," "America," "Greensleeves," and "Frere Jacques." Or, they could investigate things that peoples in various parts of the world have borrowed from Indians, such as tobacco, potatoes, corn, snowshoes, and lacrosse. Secondary students could divide their efforts. The girls might examine foods and cooking techniques, wearing apparel, and forms of beautification such as the wearing of eye shadow. The boys could look into tools and construction techniques, and sports such as track, wrestling, football, tennis, and skiing.

Or, the teacher might deal with this generalization by having students study American influences on many other cultures. He could initiate this brief exploration by filling a bulletin board with pictures of the "American touch" all over the world. The collection might include photographs of a baseball game in Japan or a basketball game at the Olympics, a "coke" stand in West Germany, a Ford car in Lima, Peru, a record hop in England, and a brightly lighted boulevard in any country. For awhile, students could continually replace old pictures with new ones.

Secondary students might benefit from a type of case study approach to this sixth fundamental insight. They could examine in depth cultural influences upon a given society over an extended period of time. Japan would be a good possibility. Prior to Commodore Matthew Perry's arrival in Tokyo Bay on July 8, 1853, Japan had closed itself off from the rest of the world for around three centuries. The story of its rapid "Westernization" is compelling. Students could try to explain why some customs in Japan have changed greatly and others have remained much the same. They could uncover some problems that have attended selected cultural changes in Japan. A humorous but revealing note could be added if students could see the play or film, *A Majority of One,* or listen to passages read from it. For symbolic purposes, the teacher might invite a salesman from a local camera shop to display and discuss a Nikon product which is world famous for its precision and performance and an example of the "Western" technological tradition at its best.

American Indians who are, of course, studied at various levels in our public schools, offer excellent opportunities for the examination of cultural diffusion and adaptation. One might point out, for example, ways in which the warlike, wandering Apache borrowed agricultural techniques from his more sedentary neighbor, the Hopi, and eventually learned to use both land and animals in a way that made his old way of life obsolete. Students might find illustrations of profound changes that have taken place in the lives of Indians whose lands proved to be rich in natural resources and who have adopted many of the white man's ways.

In his brilliant study of Mexican life entitled *Five Families,* Oscar Lewis offers the perceptive high school teacher a number of ways in which to probe the effects of one culture upon another. The following excerpt from his study describes a Catholic religious ceremony practiced by one of the families:

Every year on November 1, the Day of the Dead for Children, Rosa prepared a special meal for her dead daughter . . . On a white cloth on the dresser she placed a votive candle in a new plate (all utensils had to be new), two little pink and white skulls made of sugar "since the dead are skulls too," sweet bread and candy, and two cups of hot milk and rice. She stood the picture of the Virgin of Guadalupe on the sewing machine and surrounded it with bananas, a jicama, bread and tortillas, a plate of limes, glasses of milk and water, flowers, and candles. Under the dresser there was some copal incense burning in a bowl of charcoal. The flowers of the dead, the water and milk were to quench the thirst of the dead soul, and the two candles were to light the way back to heaven. Otherwise the child would have to use her own finger as a taper . . .[22]

Following the reading, the class might be asked to look for elements in the ritual that might be local in nature. Possibly some children of the Catholic faith might investigate the origins of this particular ceremony. They might attempt to learn whether or not it is practiced by Catholics in *all* parts of the world or only in certain areas. The teacher might point out that Rosa's family is of Indian background and ask the class to think about the possible blending of Indian and Christian ways of worship.

Finally, the teacher might attempt to let his class apply this understanding to a series of other situations. He might describe, for example, an island society in the South Seas. Some time could be spent studying the basic lifeways of the people before World War II. The class could then try to make some intelligent guesses concerning the possible impact of the arrival of American troops. Finally, the teacher could read a few authoritative descriptions of what did, in fact take place.

7. Every Cultural System Is Composed of an Interconnected Network of Behavioral Patterns; No System Is Ever Completely Static; Changes in One Area Generally Lead to Alterations in Other Segments of the System.

Rarely does one element in a culture change without bringing about modifications in other elements. Many anthropologists view a society as analogous to a complex living organism in which a change in one organ invariably and ultimately affects the entire organism. President John F. Kennedy's tragic death, for example, touched the lives not only of members of his immediate family but of people all over the United States and even many parts of the world. The passage of the Civil Rights Bill of 1964 obviously has had and will continue to have far-reaching effects on American society as a whole.

---

[22] New York: Basic Books, Inc., 1959, p. 84.

Children and youth should realize that change is an inevitability of life—anticipated or unanticipated, welcomed or unwelcomed. It is also for them to recognize that an innovation in one dimension of a culture may have significant effects on other aspects as well.

There are many stories that the teacher could read to his children or have them read which might help them look more carefully at the idea of change. Washington Irving's *Sketch Book* story, "Rip Van Winkle," is an obvious selection, for it deals in part with changes the old man observed after sleeping for twenty years. Having discussed Rip's experience, pupils might be asked to project changes they might see in their country and world if they were to return after an extended sleep.

Children might also interview their grandparents or other older people about what life was like when they were young. In class, each child could share what he found out. The teacher could stimulate further discussion and give it even more focus by asking questions such as these:

What have you learned about things older people did when they were children?

Do you do the same things they did?

Why do you suppose that you do so many things differently?

Would you like to have been a child then? Why or why not?

How did the older people you talked to feel about things that are different today?

Do you think that *your* children will do the very same things you are doing? Why?

Why do things change?

The idea of change can be further clarified through an investigation of words. The teacher might provide individual students with new dictionaries and old ones, suggesting that they find "old" words that no longer appear in current dictionaries and "new" words that cannot be seen in former editions. Or, students may be challenged to uncover coined words that have been originated to identify emerging ideas, inventions, processes, and the like. Words such as "television," "ultrasonic," and "monorail" are examples. On a still higher conceptual level, a local theologian or a philologist from the nearest college or university might be brought in as a resource person to talk about word and language changes through the ages. Students would learn as an aspect of this presentation that the same word may acquire different meanings from time to time.

As youngsters study their own country, modifications in the concept of time itself are interesting and enlightening. Pupils could be given bus, railroad, and plane schedules; asked to call the telephone company for the time; and questioned as to whether they have second hands on their wristwatches. Through a brief exchange of ideas, someone might point out that there is a great deal of emphasis today on precise time for countless operations. The teacher could ask then whether this has always been true in our country. The class might be encouraged to read about this at home and to be ready to discuss it the next day. The children would find that pioneers talked often in terms of months or seasons; that stagecoach trips were estimated in days; and so on. The history-making landing of the Ranger 7 spacecraft on the moon—a masterpiece of timing—would dramatize the change that has taken place in America's approach to time.

The teacher might ask students to thumb through old newspapers, magazines, and mail order catalogs to note the myriad forms of change evident there. Or, he could duplicate portions of older publications and use them to start discussion.

The following classified ads, first printed around 1800, might be typical of the sort of material the teacher would find useful:

NOTICE

Next Friday I shall commence for one week to occupy the barber shop in the Tavern for the purpose of *Repairing Teeth.* I travel over the entire Massachusetts area, and shall not return here for one year. *Without Pain* in the *Operation* I clean and mend teeth. I am proficient in substituting Teeth from a *Single Tooth* to a complete set, in such a manner as cannot be distinguished by close inspection from those of the *Natural Growth.*

R. Browne, Dentist

TO BE SOLD on board the Ship Bance Land, on Tuesday the 6th of May next, at Ashley Ferry; a choice cargo of about 250 fine healthy

NEGROES,

just arrived from the Windward & Rice Coast.—The utmost care has already been taken, and shall be continued, to keep them free from the least danger of being infected with the SMALL-POX, no boat having been on board, and all other communication with people from Charles-Town prevented.

Austin, Laurense & Appleby.

Older students might be invited to explore the nature and importance of change on a more intuitive basis. They would be given two or three weeks to gather information individually and to write creative papers. The teacher would answer procedural questions and help students locate information they request, but he would not give them any specific suggestions on content *per se*. Below is an illustration of the type of situation the teacher might originate:

It is November 5, 2174. This is an historic occasion for all of the earth's inhabitants. Four years ago, a world housing conference involving all of the nations of the world experiencing population problems was called. A research group composed of top scientists, engineers, architects, doctors, health and sanitation experts, nutrition specialists, and others from many parts of the globe was formed and financed by participating nations. It was proposed that a totally new kind of city be designed which would house a large number of people in a limited amount of space and in a place that had been considered as "uninhabitable" because of its climate, soil, remoteness, etc.

Today, the doors to the new city will be opened, and it will be occupied by pioneers from many countries who have volunteered to live there for a minimum of three years and perhaps a lifetime if the experiment is successful. It appears that many technical problems have been solved. The city is under a glass dome; has air conditioning throughout; employs solar energy; reclaims salt water delivered through pipelines from the ocean; has special chemical "gardens" that can grow very rapidly the foods needed; etc.

You are an anthropologist who has been invited to live with the inhabitants of "The City of the World," as it has been called. There is no form of government prescribed, no over-all religion, no uniform system of laws, no set of traditions.

What are some of the challenges the people will face, problems that will confront them, changes in behavior and values you may observe, etc.?

There are many ways that a teacher might help his students to understand that a change in one part of a cultural system could lead to alterations in other segments of that system. Primary youngsters, for example, could be asked whether they have any new brothers or sisters at home. With children in this age group, there is a good chance that they are familiar with what the arrival of a baby can do to transform many aspects of family living. They would be encourged to think of as many differences in things at home as possible that have resulted from this single change. Individual pupils might mention points such as these:

My mother has more work—getting the baby's bottle ready, changing him, washing his diapers, and things like that.

My daddy does not have as much time for me as he did before. He helps my mom feed and rock the baby.

I don't have my very own room any more.

We don't go for rides in the car as often as we used to.

More people come to visit us to see our new baby.

We eat dinner at all sorts of times now.

Class members could then be stimulated to think of other isolated items that have brought about broader changes in their lives. In a lumbering area, for instance, lack of rainfall with its attendant forest-fire danger could mean the closing down of logging operations, extended unemployment, a business slump, budget-saving meals, foregoing a birthday party, and so on.

Another technique, suitable for use with students in the intermediate and junior high school years, would be to give each pupil a 3″ x 5″ card with the name of a single invention on it. Each young person would be expected to uncover some intellectual, social, political, economic, and aesthetic side effects of the invention and to share the results of his research with his peers in the classroom. The printing press, the telescope, the cotton gin, the steam engine, the oil well, the electric motor, the telephone, the refrigerator, and the atomic reactor are obvious examples of inventions that could be used. If students have a tendency to talk only about positive outcomes of inventions, the teacher could ask whether any problems have attended given inventions. In the case of the internal combustion engine, for example, pupils may arrive at the realization that automobile accidents, injuries, and fatalities, carbon monoxide fumes in cities such as Los Angeles, and a possible decrease in the unity of the family should be taken into consideration.

Another activity related to this seventh basic insight could be developed out of actual anthropological research. The teacher could look for studies of various cultures where the general way of life has been greatly influenced by the modification, discovery, development, or loss of a specific factor. A natural resource, crop, product, process, idea, or belief could be involved. The teacher might then draft a careful description of the culture and this single dimension which he would read aloud to his class or duplicate for class use. An excellent example of the kind of material the teacher might use is this description by anthropologist Lauriston Sharp, written after his field work with a group of Australian aborigines.

Like other Australian aboriginals, the Yir Yoront group at the mouth of the Coleman River on the west coast of tropical Cape

York Peninsula originally had no knowledge of metals. Technologically their culture was of the old stone age or paleolithic type; they supported themselves by hunting and fishing, obtaining vegetable foods and needed materials from the bush by simple gathering techniques. Their only domesticated animal was the dog, and they had no domesticated plants of any kind. Unlike some other aboriginal groups, however, the Yir Yoront did have polished stone axes hafted in short handles, and these implements were most important in their economy.

The production of a stone axe required a number of simple skills. With the idea of the axe in its various details well in mind, the adult men—and only the adult men—could set about producing it, a task not considered appropriate for women or children.

The use of stone axe as a piece of capital equipment for the production of other goods indicates its very great importance in the subsistence economy of the aboriginal.

The stone they used comes from known quarries four hundred miles to the south.

Thus trading relations, which may extend the individual's personal relationships out beyond the boundaries of his own group, are associated with two of the most important items in a man's equipment, spears and axes.

The stone axe was an important symbol of masculinity among the Yir Yoront (just as pants or pipes are among ourselves). By a complicated set of ideas which we would label "ownership" the axe was defined as "belonging" to males . . .[23]

Suddenly, through increasing contact with Europeans, *steel* axes were introduced into the Yir Yoront culture. The teacher would provide no information past this point and would ask his students to write out what they think might be the projected consequences of this single change. Later, the students' ideas would be compared with actual developments.

With high school seniors, the teacher might read excerpts from fiction works such as John Steinbeck's *The Pearl* or Mark Twain's "The £1,000,000 Bank-Note" to get at this anthropological generalization. Steinbeck's novel revolves around a poor fisherman's discovery of a large, exceedingly valuable pearl. In this passage, the fisherman imagines how the pearl could change his life:

In the pearl he saw how they were dressed—Juana in a shawl stiff with newness and a new skirt, and from under the long skirt

---

[23] In Goldschmidt, *op. cit.*, pp. 158–62. This selection by Lauriston Sharp was taken from "Steel Axes for Stone Age Australians," in *Human Problems in Technological Change,* Edward H. Spicer (ed.) (New York: Russell Sage Foundation, 1952).

Kino could see that she wore shoes. It was in the pearl—the picture glowing there. He himself was dressed in new white clothes, and he carried a new hat—not of straw but of fine black felt—and he too wore shoes—not sandals but shoes that laced. But Coyotito—he was the one—he wore a blue sailor suit from the United States and a little yachting cap such as Kino had seen once when a pleasure boat put into the estuary. All of these things Kino saw in the lucent pearl and he said, "We will have new clothes."

Then to the lovely gray surface of the pearl came the little things Kino wanted: a harpoon to take the place of the one lost a year ago, a new harpoon of iron with a ring in the end of the shaft; and—his mind could hardly make the leap—a rifle—but why not, since he was rich. And Kino saw Kino in the pearl, Kino holding a Winchester carbine. It was the wildest daydreaming and very pleasant. His lips moved hesitantly over this—"A rifle," he said, "Perhaps a rifle."[24]

The pearl does change Kino's life, but not as he hoped it would. Twain's story, too, has the introduction of a single factor, again financial, into a man's life but ends in an optimistic, fairy-tale fashion. Greatly digested, it goes something like this:

As a product of a wager between two elderly brothers, a young man without any money is entrusted with a million pound bank note for thirty days. Within a week he is handsomely dressed and lavishly housed in a private hotel. Soon he is the talk of all of London. He dines with nobility and falls in love with a beautiful girl at a dinner party. By the end of the month he has accumulated a million dollars of his own and won the hand of the girl without ever cashing the bank note.[25]

8. *Personal Perceptions, Predispositions, and Values Complicate Man's Study of Man.*

It is extremely difficult for one human being to observe, report, and analyze the overt behavior of another person in a wholly objective fashion. Socrates advised, "Know thyself," yet self-knowledge is not easily achieved. If an individual cannot identify and understand many of his own motivations, characteristics, actions, and judgments, how can he hope to capture the "real" essence of some other person? Newlyweds quarreling for the first time, in-laws arguing over names proposed for first-born, and teenagers pleading

---

[24] From *The Pearl*, pp. 36–37, by John Steinbeck. Copyright © 1945 by John Steinbeck. Reprinted by permission of The Viking Press, Inc.
[25] In *The Complete Short Stories of Mark Twain*, Charles Neider (ed.) (New York: Bantam Books, Inc., 1957), pp. 316–34.

with parents for new extensions of apron strings make one wonder whether genuine communication is possible even among family members. Can any person surmount the social, economic, educational, religious, ethnic, racial, traditional, legal, moral, ideological, and national barriers erected by individuals, groups, and societies? Are objectivity, receptivity, sensitivity, and empathy possible anywhere, at any level?

We believe that an exposure to some fundamentals of anthropology should include a feeling for the tremendous tasks facing an anthropologist. The activities described here do not presume to teach youngsters how to conduct even the simplest form of anthropological research. We are not sure whether this is desirable or possible. Rather, we hope only to impress children and youth with the patience, ingenuity, objectivity, and scholarship demanded of a trained anthropologist.

Through a book, film, series of photographs, recording, or actual observation, pupils at various developmental levels might be exposed to a short sequence of behavior unfamiliar to them. A form of play or work; a festival or holiday activity; a speech or dramatic rendering; a spectator event; a political function; or an installation, inauguration, coronation, or a religious ceremony could be selected. Following the audio-visual activity, each pupil would be encouraged to describe what he heard and/or saw. The class would be instructed to make reports as factual and objective as possible—trying to avoid explanation, interpretation, or value judgments. Immediately after the discussion, the teacher would fill in the behavioral sequence with additional information he has gathered. Students would be then challenged to find errors in perception or evidence of cultural bias in their reports. The audio-visual activity would be repeated next, and a brief, refined, careful restatement made by the group.

A second possibility would be for the teacher to have his pupils suggest various attitudes that have been shaped by their culture. The children might offer statements like these:

> You should work hard so you can get ahead and make something of yourself.
> You should save your money. You might need it later· for something important.
> You should be kind and polite to older people.
> You should always tell the truth.
> You should always be on time.
> You should be a good sport and never be a bad loser.
> You should be quiet in class.

You should take your turn.
You should love your country.

Taking the statement in which the class shows the most interest (or letting each pupil choose one that appeals to him), the teacher might make the following assignment for individual work in class or at home:

Copy your sentence off the board and then answer these questions:

1. What does this sentence mean to you?
2. Have you ever thought about this idea? Do you think it is' really important? (Why? Why not?) Do you always do what this sentence tells you to do (Why? Why not?)
3. Who taught you about this idea and when? Where did the person or persons who taught you about this idea learn about it?
4. Do all of the people in our country believe this idea is important? (Why? Why not?)
5. Is this a new idea? Where did it come from? Has it always been the same or has it changed from time to time?

Dependent upon the maturity of the class and subject to various levels of understanding, the teacher might lead his students to a number of important insights. Pupils might see that they believe many things they have never considered carefully. They may point out that there are some inconsistencies in their behavior and try to explain why this may occur. They may find that various agencies (the family, school, church, peer group, etc.) support each other on some of the same ideas but may have different or even conflicting approaches to other understandings or beliefs. Students may discover that certain values are viewed as important in *their* homes but not in the homes of other students attending the same school. They may learn that some ideas are relatively new and others very old. They should realize that many "American" precepts have come from all over the world. With given ideas, they will learn that changes have taken place through the years. (For example, in early "blab" schools, children were supposed to study their lessons out loud so the teacher could be sure all of them were working. Quiet was viewed with suspicion.) They may be able to explain some of these changes but be unable to find a rationale for others.

Through all of this, students should be able to look more perceptively and objectively at things they say and do. They may see how hard it is to examine their *own* culture—let alone the cultures of others. They may be more apt to defer snap explanations and judgments. If the approach outlined here proves to be fruitful, the teacher might move the class into an investigation of some persisting idea in another culture which contrasts with one they have listed. Again, the point would be to understand the idea and to represent it faithfully, not to negate or ridicule it.

There are a variety of books that older students might read to understand how man has become attracted to the study of man; the ways in which he has attempted to conduct this study; and some of the problems he has encountered in his efforts to gather, organize, treat, and analyze data objectively. Highly technical sources should be avoided at this stage. Perhaps one of the most suitable books to convey the idea here and to attract student readers with its touch of adventure is Thor Heyerdahl's *Kon-Tiki*.[26] (The paperback edition sells for only 50¢.) Through this book, students can move from the thought that struck the author—that the huge stone figures in Tiki's jungle were similar to those left by extinct civilizations in South America—to the voyage and the author's observations. If nothing else, students should be impressed with what this group of men endured to test an hypothesis!

Still another way to help students see different levels of objectivity, sophistication, and training related to man's study of man would be for the teacher to launch a total-class search for many published legends, stories, descriptions, reports, diaries, autobiographies, etc., written by poets, arm-chair authors, explorers, soldiers, sea captains, traders, missionaries, physicians, ambassadors, and anthropologists. A "must" in this group would be *The Travels of Marco Polo*. (There is also a 50¢ paperback edition of this work.[27]) In this book, students will find fascinating mixtures of the objective and the subjective, the factual and the legendary, the empathic and the intolerant. They should be on the lookout for blanket statements about entire groups of people labeling them as "unprincipled," "treacherous," "indifferent," and so on. They should ponder the legend of the cobbler whose faith literally moved a mountain; the report of the destructive, illusory evil spirits in the desert; and the magic of the sorcerers at the banquet who could fill beverage cups spontaneously and make the cups move through the air to the hand of the Great Khan. They should notice how Marco Polo dismisses an entire province with less than a hundred words, pointing out that

26 New York: Pocket Books, Inc., 1950.
27 Milton Rugoff (ed.) (New York: The New American Library of World Literature, Inc., 1961).

there is "nothing further that is worthy to note." On the other hand, they should see his ability to note things of interest and beauty in various settings and to appreciate the organizational, administrative, husbandry, hunting, and other skills of the people whom he observed and with whom he sometimes lived and worked.

A senior high school teacher with an alert, highly-motivated class might like to give his students a feeling for the complexity of man's study of man by initiating a project whereby the class would study the school as a society. Students would pretend to be an anthropological field research team sent from another country to study adolescent behavior in an American educational institution. The class would identify areas of study such as classroom work, recess behavior, varsity and intra-mural athletics, assemblies, eating practices, language patterns, rites of passage, initiation rites, clubs, cliques, and so on. The society's name could be coined, such as the "Washingtonians" for the Washington High School. Factual data would be gathered through reviewing yearbooks; interviewing administrators, teachers, coaches, and students; observing phenomena in an anecdotal fashion; and so on. Again, the idea is not to teach research technique, by any means, but merely to give students a chance to see how difficult it is to look at human behavior as a fact instead of something to be assessed immediately by one's own value system. The style of reporting employed might follow this sample:

> The Washingtonians seem to place great value on physical activity and prowess. Approximately every two weeks they hold an athletic contest. Students who play on the "team," called the "Colonials," are regarded as important. At the end of the school year, these athletes receive a large red W which is affixed to a white sweater and worn by them. Etc.

Every community presents some opportunities for anthropological learning. Children and youth can try to look at many aspects of their community in an objective fashion. In addition to events pertinent to cultural anthropology, they may even find that some systematic archaeological research is being carried out in the community. For example, after three weeks of digging, Minnesota Historical Society archaeologists quite recently discovered foundations and artifacts of "Cantonment New Hope" on the south bank of the Minnesota River near the west end of Pike Island. The camp was constructed in 1819. Large numbers of the troops died of malaria and scurvy in the swampy area and from exposure and bad food during the winter. The cantonment was soon abandoned. It crumbled, decayed, and was finally lost to view as spring floods covered it with silt. Students could observe how a find such as this is handled. With proper arrangements, some students might even be permitted to help in a large dig, under the direction of an archaeologist. At this stage, the important thing is for them to become involved a bit in the study of man.

CONCLUSION

Cora DuBois, writing in her now classic study, *The People of Alor,* concludes that:

It is a truism in science that the more one knows, the more intricate are the problems that arise. Anthropomorphism and ethnocentrism are only on the verge of being transcended, even in science. Doors have only been opened to unbuilt rooms.[28]

Possibly this book has succeeded in opening some doors for its readers. No single volume can deal adequately with the complex field of anthropology, and we do not pretend to have done so here. On the other hand, we sincerely hope that some of anthropology's basic concepts, insights, and revelations have been clarified and vivified in this brief treatise.

We live in a time when man desperately needs to understand his fellows. His future depends upon such knowledge. In a very real sense, culture is the hope of mankind. As Malinowski put it, "Culture gives freedom to man in that it allows him to control his destinies."[29] If cruelty, bigotry, selfishness, and insensitivity were genetically passed on from parent to child, generation through generation, we might well despair of ever improving the human condition. Fortunately, this is not the case. The people inhabiting this planet are quite capable of changing their patterns of behavior and, hopefully, of enriching the quality of living for all. Whether or not man accepts this responsibility and opportunity is a crucial question of our age.

[28] Cambridge, Mass.: Harvard University Press, 1960, p. xxvii.
[29] Bronislaw Malinowski, *Freedom and Civilization* (New York: Roy Publishers, Inc., 1944), p. 319.

Index